LIGUORI CHRISTIAN INITIATION

FOR ADULTS

ENLIGHTENMENT AND MYSTAGOGY LEADER GUIDE

Journey of Faith for Adults Enlightenment and Mystagogy Leader Guide (827174)

Imprimi Potest: Stephen T. Rehrauer, CSsR, Provincial, Denver Province, the Redemptorists

Imprimatur: "In accordance with CIC 827, permission to publish has been granted on November 30, 2016, by the Rev. Msgr. Mark S. Rivituso, Vicar General, Archdiocese of St. Louis. Permission to publish is an indication that nothing contrary to Church teaching is contained in this work. It does not imply any endorsement of the opinions expressed in the publication; nor is any liability assumed by this permission."

Journey of Faith © 1993, 2005, 2016 Liguori Publications, Liguori, MO 63057.

To order, visit Liguori.org or call 800-325-9521.

Liguori Publications, a nonprofit corporation, is an apostolate of the Redemptorists. To learn more about the Redemptorists, visit Redemptorists.com. All rights reserved. No part of this publication may be reproduced, distributed, stored, transmitted, or posted in any form by any means without prior written permission.

Contributing writers and editors of 2016 *Journey of Faith for Adults Enlightenment and Mystagogy Leader Guide*: Denise Bossert, Joan McKamey, and Theresa Nienaber. Design: Lorena Mitre Jimenez. Images: Shutterstock.

Unless noted, Scripture texts in this work are taken from *New American Bible*, revised edition © 2010, 1991, 1986, 1970 Confraternity of Christian Doctrine, Washington, D.C., and are used by permission of the copyright owner. All Rights Reserved. No part of the *New American Bible* may be reproduced in any form without permission in writing from the copyright owner. Excerpts from English translation of the *Catechism of the Catholic Church for the United States of America* © 1994 United States Catholic Conference, Inc. —*Libreria Editrice Vaticana*; English translation of the *Catechism of the Catholic Church: Modifications from the Editio Typica* © 1997 United States Catholic Conference, Inc. —*Libreria Editrice Vaticana*. Compliant with The *Roman Missal*, Third Edition. *Modern Catholic Dictionary* by Fr. John A. Hardon, SJ © 1999 Eternal Life.

Printed in the United States of America.
20 19 18 17 16 / 5 4 3 2 1
Third Edition

Contents

Enlightenment and Mystagogy: A Review

The Period of Purification and Enlightenment 4

Rites and Sacraments During the Period of Enlightenment 4

Practical Suggestions 6

The Period of Postbaptismal Catechesis or Mystagogy 6

Effective Catechesis during Mystagogy 7

Transitioning Into the Parish Community 7

Enlightenment Lesson Plans

E1: Election: Saying Yes to Jesus

E2: Living Lent

E3: Scrutinies: Looking Within

E4: The Creed

E5: The Way of the Cross

E6: The Lord's Prayer

E7: The Meaning of Holy Week

E8: Easter Vigil Retreat

Mystagogy Lesson Plans

M1: Conversion: A Lifelong Process

M2: The Role of the Laity

M3: Your Spiritual Gifts

M4: Discernment

M5: Our Call to Holiness

M6: Living the Virtues

M7: Family Life

M8: Evangelization

Enlightenment and Mystagogy Glossary 104

Enlightenment and Mystagogy: A Review

The Period of Purification and Enlightenment

Since the earliest centuries, the Church has set aside the season of Lent as a particular time for repentance, conversion, and preparation for the sacraments. The RCIA process and celebration of baptism is centered on the Easter Vigil, with the rites of election and calling, scrutinies, and entire catechumenate scheduled in relation to that feast (*RCIA* 17, 20–26; *CCC* 1168; *CIC* 856).

Because repentance and conversion require personal and internal preparation, the *Journey of Faith for Adults, Enlightenment* lessons focus on guided, prayerful reflection. The lessons will assist the participants in their internal preparation for the sacraments, and encourage them to live out their faith in hands-on ways.

"[Enlightenment] is a period of more intense spiritual preparation, consisting more in interior reflection than in catechetical instruction, and is intended to purify the minds and hearts of the elect as they search their own consciences and do penance" (*RCIA* 139).

While the elect do not fully possess the graces and gifts of discipleship during the period of purification and enlightenment, they should feel ownership of their Christian faith. Baptized candidates, as members of the Christian Church, should begin to identify themselves as Catholic and express their faith in keeping with sacred Tradition.

The sessions and events during the enlightenment period should allow participants to experience Lent along with the parish community, whose members are also undergoing spiritual renewal and preparing to celebrate the paschal mystery more deeply (*RCIA* 138). At the Easter Vigil, the faithful will renew their baptismal vows as the participants profess their faith in Christ and the Catholic Church. This unity and integration will grow throughout the period of mystagogy, which usually corresponds to the Easter season.

Rites and Sacraments During the Period of Enlightenment

The enlightenment and purification period begins with the rite of election. Please refer to the *Catechumenate Leader Guide* and other *Journey of Faith for Adults* materials for details.

The Scrutinies

Rather than examination, interrogation, or harsh judgment, "the scrutinies…are rites for self-searching and repentance," designed "to inspire in the elect a desire for purification and redemption" (*RCIA* 141, 143). The prayers and intercessions encourage the elect to strive for the narrow gate (Matthew 7:13–14; Luke 13:24–28). Through the exorcisms, they "are freed from the effects of sin and from the influence of the devil" (*RCIA* 144). Having previously been instructed in the nature of sin and expressed their desire and commitment to receive the sacraments of initiation, participants are strengthened and sent forth to make their discipleship a reality.

The questions, activities, journal prompts, and other material in these lessons help to prepare each participant for this stage in their faith journey. The bishop or priest will "question the candidates individually" in the formula for the profession of faith at the Easter Vigil (*RCIA* 224–25). Should participants express doubts or concerns about their conversion, meet with them privately to determine what additional support can be provided.

The Presentations

The *Presentation of the Creed* should be celebrated during the week following the first scrutiny and, whenever possible, within a Mass so that the faith community may be present (*RCIA* 157; *CIC* 837). It prepares the elect to memorize the Creed, for the *Recitation of the Creed* (see Preparation Rites), and to profess their faith on the day of their baptism (*RCIA* 148).

During the *Presentation of the Creed*:

- The prescribed readings, which replace the regular weekday readings, are proclaimed during the Liturgy of the Word (*RCIA* 158).
- After the homily, the priest calls the elect forward to receive the words and mysteries of the Creed. The Nicene or Apostles' Creed may be used, depending on the parish's tradition (*RCIA* 160).
- The priest begins to recite the Creed, and the assembly joins in.
- The priest prays over the elect and dismisses them prior to the Liturgy of the Eucharist. If they are to stay, he reminds them that they cannot participate fully, but that they remain "as a sign of our hope that all God's children will eat and drink with the Lord…" (*RCIA* 163).

The *Presentation of the Lord's Prayer* should be celebrated during the week following the third scrutiny or in the preparation rites. It prepares the elect to make the prayer their own as they join the congregation in praying it prior to their first Eucharist (*RCIA* 149).

During the *Presentation of the Lord's Prayer*:

- The prescribed readings, which replace the regular weekday readings, are proclaimed during the Liturgy of the Word (*RCIA* 179).

- Just prior to the Gospel reading, the deacon or assisting minister calls the elect forward. Matthew's Gospel account of the Lord's Prayer is proclaimed.

- After the homily, the priest prays over the elect: "Deepen the faith and understanding of these elect, chosen for baptism. Give them new birth…so that they may be numbered among your adopted children" (*RCIA* 182).

- The priest dismisses the elect prior to the Liturgy of the Eucharist.

Preparation Rites on Holy Saturday

The number and arrangement of these rites will depend on the needs of your elect, timing and ability, and other factors (*RCIA* 185–86). The Church offers the following model for your benefit (*RCIA* 187–92):

1. Begin with an appropriate gathering song.

2. The celebrant greets everyone with a suitable formula or words.

3. Scripture readings are chosen from the rites and proclaimed, with psalms or hymns in between if needed.

4. The celebrant gives a brief homily or explanation of the texts.

5. The various rites are celebrated. These may include the *Presentation of the Lord's Prayer*, the *Recitation of the Creed*, the *Ephphetha rite*, and/or the rite of *Choosing a Baptismal Name*.

6. The celebrant concludes with the prayer of blessing and dismissal.

The Easter Vigil

The feast of Easter, in particular the Easter Vigil liturgy, is the highlight of the Church year. Given its prominence and his prerogative to initiate (baptize) those fourteen years old or older, the bishop is the preferred celebrant (*RCIA* 207; *CIC* 863). "Adult candidates, including children of catechetical age, are to receive baptism, confirmation, and Eucharist in a single eucharistic celebration" (*National Statutes for the Catechumenate*, 14). This trifecta of sacraments is a distinct feature of the RCIA process and reflects the unified nature of Christian initiation (*CIC* 842).

If mixed groups of the elect and baptized candidates are to celebrate the sacraments together, "the condition and status of those already baptized should be carefully respected and distinguished" (*National Statutes* 26, 33–34). Whenever this is the case, your RCIA process should reflect the difference between these two groups from the beginning. Continuing it through the Easter Vigil should not be hard. The bishop or priest may already have solutions.

The Vigil Mass and sacraments of initiation are discussed in the *Journey of Faith Inquiry Leader Guide*, lesson C1: *The RCIA Process and Rites*, and lesson E7: *The Meaning of Holy Week*. You may also refer to *RCIA* 206–43 and *Lectionary* no. 41. Additional steps and points are detailed here:

- The celebration of baptism begins with a presentation of the elect with their godparents, and a litany of the saints.

- The celebrant blesses and prays over the baptismal waters.

- The elect renounce sin and make a profession of faith. "Adults are not saved unless they come forward of their own accord and the will to accept God's gift through their own belief. The faith of those to be baptized is not simply the faith of the Church, but the personal faith of each one of them…" (*RCIA* 211).

- The elect are baptized, preferably by immersion (*National Statutes for the Catechumenate*, 17). Whether baptism is by full or partial immersion or simply by pouring, it should "take on its full importance as the sign of that mystical sharing in Christ's death and resurrection through which those who believe in his name die to sin and rise to eternal life.…This washing is not a mere purification rite but the sacrament of being joined to Christ" (*RCIA* 213).

- The newly baptized are anointed with oil and clothed in a white garment. Godparents are presented with a candle lit from the Easter candle.

- The celebrant invites the newly baptized to receive confirmation. Afterward, the assembled faithful renew their baptismal promises. If the combined rite is used, the renewal will come first, followed by confirmation.
- Previously baptized candidates then come forward and profess their faith. The sacrament of confirmation is conferred with the laying on of hands and anointing with chrism.
- As the Liturgy of the Eucharist begins, neophytes should take part in the procession of the gifts to the altar (*RCIA* 241). The entire RCIA group and its supporters—neophytes, leaders, catechists, sponsors, godparents, and family members—should receive the Eucharist under both forms (*RCIA* 243, 594).

Practical Suggestions

- Prepare the RCIA team, participants, sponsors, and godparents for the rites of sending, election, and/or calling prior to the beginning of Lent. If Lent is early, you may have to adjust the catechumenate period accordingly. Lesson *E1: Election: Saying Yes to Jesus* is specifically designed for this purpose.
- Help the elect and candidates enter the Lenten season as deeply as possible. Present lesson *E2: Living Lent* early in the season. It provides a context and offers suggestions for the season. Attend the Ash Wednesday service as an RCIA group, and incorporate Lenten readings, themes, prayers, and sacramentals into the sessions. Distribute a daily Lenten devotional or activity and encourage godparents and sponsors to discuss it with participants regularly.
- Arrange a time in the church, chapel, or a nearby shrine where the RCIA group can pray, even walk, the stations together using lesson *E5: The Way of the Cross*. Assign individuals to announce the stations, proclaim the Scriptures, and read the reflections and prayers aloud.
- Schedule the remaining enlightenment lessons to correspond with their respective rites or celebrations. Present lesson *E3: Scrutinies: Looking Within* before the third Sunday of Lent and lessons *E4: The Creed* and *E6: The Lord's Prayer* before the presentations. Lesson *E7: The Meaning of Holy Week* can be presented on or before Palm Sunday. Lesson *E8: Easter Vigil Retreat* should be presented as close to the Easter Vigil as possible.
- Arrange a special celebration of reconciliation for the baptized candidates prior to the Easter Vigil (*National Statutes* 27). Whether these individuals are non-Catholics celebrating their first penance or uncatechized Catholics returning to the sacrament after many years, make sure they receive proper preparation, instruction, and support. Strongly encourage their leaders, catechists, sponsors, godparents, and baptized family and friends to attend as well. If the group is large, it may be better to schedule this event separately from regular reconciliation times.
- During the Easter Vigil, baptized candidates should come forward for confirmation after the baptism of the elect is completed. Have previously baptized candidates stand together, to distinguish their different sacramental status.
- Celebrate with the parish community after the Easter Vigil or during the Easter octave, but reserve any closing or final celebrations for after mystagogy (Pentecost) to reflect the unfinished nature of the RCIA process at Easter. Incorporate the communal, covenantal, and evangelistic themes of Pentecost into your festivities (See *RCIA* 249).

The Period of Postbaptismal Catechesis or Mystagogy

The words *mystagogy* and *mystery* share a Greek root meaning "initiated person." With this last period of the RCIA process, the Church recognizes the need for continuing and deepening support for the newly baptized. Although they have been formed and converted, there is still much to learn from the Church and the full experience of Catholic living: "The faith required for Baptism is not a perfect or mature faith, but a beginning that is called to develop….For all the baptized, children or adults, faith must grow *after* Baptism" (*CCC* 1253–54; see also *RCIA* 245).

The Church sets aside the Easter season as the ideal time to delve into the mysteries of our faith, the sacraments, and the Church (*RCIA* 247). During these fifty days, the Sunday liturgies should specially focus on the new members of the body of Christ, and the people of the parish should extend themselves in welcoming their new brothers and sisters. The readings from the Acts of the Apostles emphasize the community and the continuing work of salvation through the ever-growing discipleship of the fledgling Church.

The mystagogy sessions should facilitate the neophytes' full participation in the sacraments and integration into the faith community. "This is a time for the community and the neophytes together to grow in deepening their grasp of the paschal mystery and in making it part of their lives through meditation on the Gospel, sharing in the Eucharist, and doing the works of charity" (*RCIA* 244). By their shared presence and fervor, they witness to the joy of the gospel and serve as examples of living disciples.

Effective Catechesis During Mystagogy

In his apostolic exhortation On Catechesis in our Time [*Catechesi Tradendae*], Pope St. John Paul II identifies several elements of catechesis. Three of them are fundamental to the period of mystagogy: "celebration of the sacraments, integration into the ecclesial community, and apostolic and missionary witness" (18; see *CCC* 6). To that Pope Francis added some practical demands of what he called "*mystagogic initiation*" (The Joy of the Gospel [*Evangelii Gaudium*], 166). These guidelines provide a framework from which you can build a meaningful period of postbaptismal catechesis:

Create a suitable environment. Give your sessions a distinctly liturgical feel. Incorporate sacred art, music, and liturgical prayers, texts, and forms whether or not they are connected to Sunday Mass.

Offer an attractive presentation. Continue to emphasize the beauty of our faith and explore how what we do reflects the joyful hope of Christ's death and resurrection.

Continue the use of eloquent symbols. Connect the liturgy and sacraments to the wonders of nature, human nature and daily life, and the participants' own experiences to deepen their meaning and value.

Include the process in a broader growth process. Emphasize that in baptism we have died to our old selves and risen to a new life. The mystagogy lessons are designed to prompt the neophytes to active discipleship.

Focus on evangelization rather than instruction. Remind everyone (including yourself) that the light of faith is present. After baptism, your job is to fan the Spirit's flame. Incorporate more listening and sharing of experiences into your sessions. When discussing Scripture, go beyond understanding the story and prompt each person to make it his or her own.

Provide opportunities for contemplation and discernment. Plan a prayer session or visit to the adoration chapel. Dedicate at least part of a session to reflecting on the Triduum and Vigil in particular. Spend ten to twenty minutes each week on the lesson questions and journal prompts.

Guide the participants toward greater initiative. If you haven't already, teach participants to lead simple prayers and to proclaim Scripture. Encourage them to share how God is working in their lives and to determine ways in which they can respond.

Transitioning Into the Parish Community

Through the sacraments of initiation, the neophytes are permanently changed (*CCC* 1272). With their newfound grace, salvation, and identity, they receive the responsibilities of discipleship and call to active participation in parish life. Yet the mysteries of the Easter Vigil impact the Church as well (*RCIA* 246). In the liturgy and reception of new members, it is refreshed, made new. The period of mystagogy is a time for neophytes and the rest of the faithful to welcome each other and to discern where God is leading them together.

As primary representatives of the community, RCIA leaders and catechists must model this new relationship and extend it to the rest of the parish and diocese. Some ways to start include making introductions, encouraging the neophytes' full participation in the Mass, and supporting their early efforts to carry the gospel to others in word, deed, and ministry.

Ways to Create Community

- *Recognize the neophytes and newly received by name.* Make the assembly aware of their presence in the community. Consider common mentions of other groups, such as the sick, recently deceased, baptized infants, and wedding banns. Follow your pastor or parish leader's instructions for requesting a special intention or spoken or written announcement.

- *Bring the Mass to them.* The Sundays of Easter are "so-called Masses for neophytes" (*RCIA* 247). This doesn't require a teaching Mass or special treatment, but they should be able to see the deep, spiritual realities happening in and around them. Having the neophytes sit together or focusing the homily on the sacraments can help.

- *Keep the Easter season.* Rather than wind down after the Easter Vigil, work with the pastor and the whole parish to take part in the ongoing marvels of Easter.

- *Create spiritual connections.* Post or print questions or material from your sessions where parishioners can access them. This gives them an experience of mystagogy and a convenient way to share reflections and discussions with their own families.

- *Allow for gradual integration.* Invite godparents, sponsors, and family to continue attending Mass with the neophytes and assisting them in their ongoing formation. Regularly exploring the parish bulletin, newsletter, or social-media feed together for events to attend are simple activities that can be done over coffee or brunch.

As the participants approach their first sacramental anniversary, you may observe the fruits of established friendships, familiarity, and a real commitment to the faith. In turn, the Church gives thanks and offers these gifts for the benefit of all, including the new group of neophytes.

E1: Election: Saying Yes to Jesus

Catechism: 422–429, 618, 2464–74

Objectives

Participants will...

- Decide how they will respond to Jesus' invitation to follow him.
- Consider the various responses to Jesus' invitation in the Gospels.
- Connect saying yes to Jesus with the *rite of election* and the signing of the book of election.

Leader Meditation

John 21:1–19

Jesus Christ has made you a fisher of men and women. The participants in your class are the fish in your net, the net you dropped at the Lord's command, the net you hauled up and have carried to shore. It is time to present the fish to the Lord. Imagine that you are Peter. Jesus is asking: Do you love me? Every day, you have the opportunity to say "yes" to the Lord. In this passage, the Lord asks Peter if Peter loves him. The first time Peter says "yes," Jesus tells Peter to feed the Lord's lambs. The second time, the Lord tells Peter to tend to the Lord's sheep. The third time, the Lord says to Peter to feed his sheep. In doing these things, Peter will act on his love for Jesus Christ. You are like Peter. In this lesson, you will bring the sheep to the Lord, and he will invite them to say yes to him. Pray for the necessary grace to lead the participants well and for sufficient grace that they will respond with a firm yes.

Related *Catholic Updates*

- "The Lord's Supper: Ancient Story, New Beginning" (C1104A)
- "'Light of Faith': Key Themes From Pope Francis' First Encyclical" (C1310A)
- "How God Invites Us to Grow: Six Stages of Faith Development" (C8710A)
- "Lent: Giving Our Hearts to God" (C9702A)

Leader Preparation

- Read the lesson handout, this lesson plan, the Scripture passage, and the *Catechism* sections.
- Obtain a recording of "Lord, I Need You" by Matt Maher, from *All The People Said Amen*, Essential Records.

Welcome

Greet participants as they arrive. Check for supplies and immediate needs. Solicit questions or comments about the previous session and/or share new information and findings. Begin promptly.

Opening Scripture

John 21:1–19

Light the candle and read the passage aloud. Share with participants that this lesson is all about Jesus "popping the question." He is proposing to us, and it is the greatest proposal of all time. He waits for our yes with more love than any bridegroom has ever had. Invite participants to think about how they would respond to Jesus' call as you begin the lesson.

> "From this loving knowledge of Christ springs the desire to proclaim him, to 'evangelize,' and to lead others to the 'yes' of faith in Jesus Christ."
>
> CCC 428

Journey of Faith for Adults, Enlightenment and Mystagogy Leader Guide

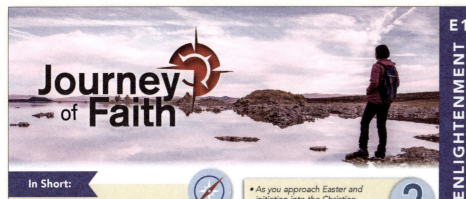

ENLIGHTENMENT — E1 — ADULTS

In Short:
- Jesus invites us to say yes to his invitation to follow him.
- The Gospels report many different responses to Jesus' invitation.
- Catechumens become the "elect" through the rite of election.

- As you approach Easter and initiation into the Christian community, it's time to examine your life in relation to what Christ asks of you. Jesus has been calling you your entire life. How have you responded to that call?
- How will you continue to respond to Christ in new and deeper ways? Where is Jesus leading you?

Election: Saying Yes to Jesus

On the first Sunday of Lent, catechumens celebrate the rite of election and enter the period of purification and enlightenment, which leads to the celebration of the Easter sacraments. *Election* comes from a word that means "choose." The ceremony reflects this theme: God has chosen and called us.

The Church community hears testimony from godparents and catechists about how the catechumens have responded to God's call. The community accepts the catechumens, who state their desire to join the Church. They write their names in the *Book of the Elect* as one of "the chosen."

Baptized Christians seeking full communion with the Catholic Church may celebrate a rite called the call to continuing conversion.

Many Are Called

Jesus invited many to become his disciples, carry on his mission, and follow the way of the cross. Some responded enthusiastically. Former disciples of John the Baptist, Galilean fishermen, tax collectors, people from every walk of life accepted his call and followed him.

But the Gospels record several incidents in which potential disciples refused to commit to Christ and let the opportunity slip away.

"I Will...but First..."

The Gospels of Matthew and Luke describe Jesus' encounter with those who say they desire to follow Jesus but not quite yet: "Lord, let me go first and bury my father" (Matthew 8:21; Luke 9:59). In Jesus' time, this meant, "Let me come after my father is dead." And this didn't necessarily mean the father was old or sick.

> "I will follow you, Lord, but first let me say farewell to my family at home."
> *Luke 9:61*

CCC 422–429, 618, 2464–74

Election: Saying Yes to Jesus

- Discuss the rite of election. Compare election to the moment a man proposes marriage, or (as not all participants will be called to marriage) to receiving a job offer. It's a formal process, and it's filled with meaning and significance. Saying "yes" sets us on a new path in life. Jesus is inviting the catechumens to a new path—the path that leads to eternal life.

- Remind participants that while the *rite of election* marks the final stage of preparation for full reception into the Church, as an engagement or job offer letter marks the beginning of a final stage of a process, it is just the beginning of a faith journey. After as wedding comes a lifelong commitment to the marriage. After accepting a job comes the day to day task of working. The process of faith and saying "yes" to Jesus does not end here.

- Offer participants time to respond to the two reflection questions in their prayer journal. Think about where Jesus has lead you, and where he is leading you now. Share any relevant experiences with the group and encourage participants to share as well.

"I Will...but First..."

- Discuss the many excuses those in the Gospel stories used to postpone their journey with Jesus.

- One man wanted to wait until his father had died, putting his perceived obligation to his father ahead of his faith (Matthew 8:21 and Luke 9:59). Another would follow the Lord only after finishing business at home (Luke 9:61).

- Emphasize that our family life, career, and personal relationships take on their true meaning only when following Christ is our highest priority. Discuss those examples from the previous question, and have participants offer scenarios where those obligations to family, work, or the home are kept while still giving Jesus a wholehearted "yes."

- Ask participants to consider their own situations of "I will but first…" Allow those who feel comfortable to share.

- Offer participants time to respond to the reflection question silently, or discuss it as a group. Think of your own example of an "I will" disciple who inspires you to share with the group. (This can be someone you know personally, or a saint you've found inspiring.)

"This Saying Is Hard…"

- Emphasize that some Church teachings will be more difficult for participants to accept than others. What is easy for one catechumen to accept may be difficult for another. What is a "hard teaching" for one may make perfect sense to another catechumen. Our "yes" is an affirmation of our trust in Christ as well as a promise to follow Christ. However, we are free to say "no" to this invitation, as did some of his disciples. Sacred Scripture is clear. The one who walks away from the invitation does so in sorrow. But Jesus Christ gives us the freedom to choose.

- Pause in the lesson and give participants an opportunity to complete the activity with a partner or their sponsor or godparent. Allow time for participants to share any new realizations or discoveries.

- Discuss the cost, and difficulty, of giving Jesus a fully realized "yes." Emphasize that the Twelve were asked to accept difficult teachings and that the Samaritan woman was asked to look critically at her own life and choices. Ask participants to reflect on the moments in their own lives Jesus is asking them to reconsider in the light of faith.

These people declared their willingness to follow Christ, but at their own convenience, on their own terms. To them, Jesus replied: "Let the dead bury their dead.…No one who sets a hand to the plow and looks to what was left behind is fit for the kingdom of God" (Luke 9:60, 62).

Those who accept Jesus' call must do so promptly, enthusiastically, and completely. The Galilean fishermen "left everything and followed him" (Luke 5:11). The tax collector, "leaving everything behind…got up and followed him" (Luke 5:28).

When Jesus came to the house of Martha and Mary in Bethany, Mary "sat beside the Lord at his feet listening to him speak" (Luke 10:39). Martha had other priorities and wanted Mary to help her, but Jesus answered, "Martha, Martha, you are anxious and worried about many things. There is need of only one thing. Mary has chosen the better part and it will not be taken from her" (Luke 10:41–42).

- What is helping you become an "I will" disciple instead of a "would be" disciple?

"This Saying Is Hard…"
In chapter 6 of John's Gospel, Jesus foreshadows his institution of the sacrament of the Eucharist:

"Whoever eats my flesh and drinks my blood has eternal life, and I will raise him on the last day. For my flesh is true food, and my blood is true drink. Whoever eats my flesh and drinks my blood remains in me and I in him."

John 6:54–56

The disciples were shocked, saying: "This saying is hard; who can accept it?" (John 6:60). When Jesus refused to modify his claims, "many [of] his disciples returned to their former way of life and no longer accompanied him" (John 6:66). As long as Jesus' teaching matched their expectations, they were content to follow. When Jesus challenged their presuppositions rather than telling them what they wanted to hear, they left him.

- How do you respond when something Jesus says makes you uncomfortable?

Choose a part of Jesus' teaching you find difficult. With your leader's or sponsor's help, find a Gospel verse that reflects this teaching. Let Jesus guide you as you read the passage:

Read the passage as you slowly breathe in and out.

1. Imagine Jesus talking to you.
2. Let him gently lead you through the teaching and address your concerns.
3. Sit in Jesus' presence and listen for his loving response.

- What are your greatest fears or doubts regarding this matter? What do you find challenging?
- How does this passage enlighten your understanding? What is Jesus saying to you?
- What steps can you take to better accept this teaching?

In contrast, when Jesus asked the Twelve, "Do you also want to leave?" Simon Peter replied, "Master, to whom shall we go? You have the words of eternal life" (John 6:67–69). The faith of the Twelve enabled them to remain disciples of Christ while others retreated, scandalized and confused.

When Jesus spoke to the Samaritan woman at the well, he said things that must have been hard to hear. Not only did he promise her living water that would keep her from thirsting but he told her that she and other Samaritans "worship what you do not understand" (John 4:22).

Most difficult of all, he laid bare her whole life. When she said she had no husband, Jesus said, "you have had five husbands, and the one you have now is not your husband" (John 4:18). She could have reacted with resentment or indignation to any of these "hard sayings." Instead, she ran to tell others that Jesus is the Messiah. Many Samaritans from that city believed in him because of the woman's testimony: "He told me everything I have done" (John 4:39). Her faith, and theirs, was deepened by hearing the truth.

"He Went Away Sad…"

Perhaps the most poignant of Jesus' conversations was with a rich young man who asked:

> "'What must I do to inherit eternal life?… All of these [commandments] I have observed from my youth.' Jesus, looking at him, loved him and said to him, 'You are lacking in one thing. Go, sell what you have, and give to [the] poor and you will have treasure in heaven; then come, follow me.' At that statement his face fell, and he went away sad, for he had many possessions."
>
> *Mark 10:17–22*

Although the young man had observed all the commandments, his first allegiance was to his wealth. It gave him a sense of identity and security.

- What gives you a sense of identity and security? How attached are you to your possessions?

The rich young man didn't realize that true identity and security come from Christ. He wasn't sure that what he'd find in Christ would compensate for surrendering his possessions. So he left saddened.

In contrast, consider the generosity of the woman who "came with an alabaster jar of perfumed oil…. and poured it on his head" (Mark 14:3). This perfume was worth "three hundred days' wages," yet that sacrifice didn't stop her. She gave generously out of love. For that reason, Jesus said, "Amen, I say to you, wherever the gospel is proclaimed to the whole world, what she has done will be told in memory of her" (Mark 14:9).

"I Do Not Know Him…"

Probably the saddest loss for Jesus came after his arrest. Just when Jesus needed his closest friends the most, they ran away. Peter, who'd sworn he would die with Jesus, denied Jesus three times: "I do not know him" (Luke 22:57). John was the only one of the Twelve Apostles who attended Jesus' crucifixion and burial.

The women were faithful despite the danger: "Standing by the cross of Jesus were his mother and his mother's sister, Mary the wife of Clopas, and Mary of Magdala" (John 19:25). "Mary Magdalene and the other Mary remained sitting there, facing the tomb" (Matthew 27:61), watching as Jesus was buried. They returned later to anoint his body and were the first to see the resurrected Jesus, the first to carry the news of Easter to the world.

- When have you been uncomfortable about sharing your choice to follow Jesus? Why?
- When have you run from the cross?

Our Response to Jesus' Call

Our Lenten liturgies and penitential practices help us explore our own readiness to respond to Christ's call. There's probably a little bit of the would-be disciple in each of us—a part of ourselves that holds on to doubt, discouragement, or confusion in our relationship to God or Church. We may be tempted to seek our security beyond Christ and his love for us. Sometimes the demands of discipleship may seem too restrictive, inconvenient, uncomfortable, or unreasonable.

When we realize we've hesitated and want to turn back, it's time to remember all the disciples who ran away and then returned. Like Peter, we can turn from "I do not know him" to "Lord, you know that I love you" (John 21:15). But we must then accept the cost of discipleship as Peter did.

There's no question that it's difficult to give an unconditional "yes" to Christ, to embrace wholeheartedly the cross he asks us to carry. But if we ask the Lord to help us make that leap of faith, abandoning the pride, insecurity, selfishness, or apathy that can cripple discipleship, we'll respond ever more generously to him.

"Let your 'yes' mean 'yes.'"

Matthew 5:37

ENLIGHTENMENT — JOURNEY OF FAITH

"I Do Not Know Him…"

- Discuss with participants the kind of situations where we can be tempted to deny Jesus or run from his teachings and ways we can reaffirm our faith in moments like these.

Our Response to Jesus' Call

- Emphasize that Jesus has been calling us for our entire lives. Participants will have felt it most clearly and acutely these past few weeks and months as they've inquired about the Church and become part of the community. Now is the time to examine their lives in relation to what Christ asks.

"He Went Away Sad…"

- As a group, discuss possible responses to the reflection question. Emphasize that when we feel our identity is tied to the things we possess it can be especially difficult to be willing to let those things go and follow Jesus.

- Things that give us a sense of security can be anything from our bank accounts, to our job, to long-term friendships, to not getting involved in difficult conversations. We can get our identity from our work, our family and our children, our position in the community, even the things we own.

- Ask participants to discuss some ways we can rediscover (or discover for the first time) the person God is calling us to become.

- Some of these ways may include an ongoing practice of prayer or spiritual journaling, meeting with a trusted Catholic advisor or spiritual director, or reading Scripture or writings from the saints.

Election: Saying Yes to Jesus

Read 2 Corinthians 1:18–20 and Luke 14:28. Reflect on your response to God's call.

- How ready am I to say, "I've calculated the cost and am ready to follow Christ?"
- What is God asking of me today (possible sacrifices, costs of discipleship)?

Journey of Faith for Adults: Enlightenment, E1 (826276)

Imprimi Potest: Stephen T. Rehrauer, CSsR, Provincial, Denver Province, the Redemptorists.
Imprimatur: "In accordance with CIC 827, permission to publish has been granted on June 7, 2016, by the Rev. Msgr. Mark Rivituso, Vicar General, Archdiocese of St. Louis. Permission to publish is an indication that nothing contrary to Church teaching is contained in this work. It does not imply any endorsement of the opinions expressed in the publication, nor is any liability assumed by this permission."

Journey of Faith © 1993, 2005, 2016 Liguori Publications, Liguori, MO 63057. To order, visit Liguori.org or call 800-325-9521. Liguori Publications, a nonprofit corporation, is an apostolate of the Redemptorists. To learn more about the Redemptorists, visit Redemptorists.com. All rights reserved. No part of this publication may be reproduced, distributed, stored, transmitted, or posted in any form by any means without prior written permission. Editors of 2016 Journey of Faith: Denise Bossert, Julia DiSalvo, and Joan McKamey. Design: Lorena Mitre Jimenez. Images: Shutterstock. Unless noted, Scripture texts in this work are taken from the *New American Bible*, revised edition © 2010, 1991, 1986, 1970 Confraternity of Christian Doctrine, Washington, D.C., and are used by permission of the copyright owner. All Rights Reserved. No part of the *New American Bible* may be reproduced in any form without permission in writing from the copyright owner. Excerpts from English translation of the *Catechism of the Catholic Church* for the United States of America © 1994 United States Catholic Conference, Inc.—Libreria Editrice Vaticana, English translation of the *Catechism of the Catholic Church: Modifications from the Editio Typica* © 1997 United States Catholic Conference, Inc.—Libreria Editrice Vaticana. Compliant with *The Roman Missal, Third Edition.* Printed in the United States of America. 20 19 18 17 16 / 5 4 3 2 1. Third Edition.

Liguori Publications — A Redemptorist Ministry

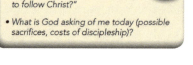

ISBN 978-0-7648-2627-6

Journey of Faith for Adults, Enlightenment and Mystagogy Leader Guide

Journaling

If you have time at the end of this session, read 2 Corinthians 1:18–20 and Luke 14:28 as a group. Then allow participants some time to silently reflect on, or write, their responses to the journal questions provided at the end of the lesson.

Closing Prayer

Play recording of "Lord, I Need You" (Matt Maher, from *All The People Said Amen*, Essential Records). End with a few moments of silence and ask for petitions. Close with this simple prayer.

> *Lord,*
> *It is a blessing to know that you are Lord, creator, and savior. You love us with an eternal love. It is difficult to comprehend this kind of love for you have given us the gift of free will, knowing that we may choose to walk away from your love or we may choose to receive this love and say yes to it. Give us the grace to say yes, for it is our heart's desire to love you, to know you, and to serve you.*
> *Amen.*

Looking Ahead

Lesson *E1: Election: Saying Yes to Jesus* is the beginning of a lifelong journey with our Lord and his Church. Each catechumen who says yes to the journey is ready to enter Lent and complete the final path to Easter Vigil. As participants prepare to enter into the Lenten season, ask them to begin examining their lives with the eyes of faith, noting areas where they could improve and offering thanksgiving for areas where they clearly see God's influence at work.

Election: Saying Yes to Jesus

E2: Living Lent

Catechism: 571–605

Objectives

Participants will...

- Consider the original purpose of Lent as a period of preparation for baptism.
- Explain the various themes of Lent, including repentance, sacrifice, and spiritual growth.
- Interpret the meaning behind the Lenten practices of fasting, prayer, and almsgiving.

Leader Meditation

Matthew 4:1–11

Recall times when you have felt you were in a desert—times that were difficult and seemingly lifeless. Why are we tempted to turn away from Christ and look for comfort elsewhere during times like these? In what places or in what things have you been tempted to find comfort? What brought you back to Christ?

Related *Catholic Updates*

- "In the Desert With Jesus: Biblical Themes of Lent" (C0502A)
- "Lent: A 40-Day Retreat, Rediscovering Your Baptismal Call" (C9002A)
- "Ash Wednesday: Our Shifting Understanding of Lent" (C0402A)
- "Lent: A Journey Into the Inner Self" (C9102A)

Leader Preparation

- Read the lesson, this lesson plan, the Scripture passage, and the Catechism sections.
- Collect some physical symbols of Lent to show participants such as ashes, palm leaves, Stations of the Cross, and so on.
- Be familiar with the vocabulary terms for this lesson: fasting, abstinence, almsgiving. Definitions are provided in this guide's glossary.

Welcome

Greet participants as they arrive. Check for supplies and immediate needs. Solicit questions or comments about the previous session and/or share new information and findings. Begin promptly.

Opening Scripture

Matthew 4:1–11

Light the candle and read the passage aloud. Ask participants to reflect on "desert experiences" in their lives. Ask if they've felt more easily tempted during these moments.

> "The event of the Cross and Resurrection abides and draws everything toward life."
>
> CCC 1085

Journey of Faith for Adults, Enlightenment and Mystagogy Leader Guide

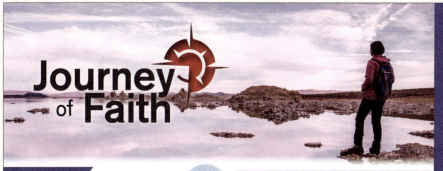

Journey of Faith

ENLIGHTENMENT — **E2**

In Short:
- Lent was originally a period of preparation for baptism.
- Lenten themes include repentance, sacrifice, and spiritual growth.
- Three traditional Lenten practices are fasting, prayer, and almsgiving.

Beginning on Ash Wednesday and ending before the Mass of the Lord's Supper on Holy Thursday, Lent is a period of about forty days, not counting Sundays. It's a penitential season of prayer, fasting, and almsgiving in preparation for the celebration of Easter.

Living Lent

We take time to prepare for things that are important to us. During Lent, we prepare for the greatest celebration of the Church year—Easter. We follow the path of Jesus, who journeyed through death to resurrection. We die to ourselves so that we, like Jesus, might rise again.

Lent is a time of preparation, a time of spiritual growth. We discard our faulty attitudes and unhealthy habits. We pick up new attitudes and fresh perspectives. The dying and rebirth that take place within our hearts reflect the paschal mystery—the suffering, death, resurrection, and ascension of our Lord.

The word *Lent* comes from an early English word that refers to the lengthening of daylight hours during spring. While the season of Lent was originally a time of final preparation for those adults being baptized at Easter, the entire Church now enters into the spirit and practices of Lent.

Lent is a good time to ask yourself:

- *What do I need to be happy?*
- *How do I spend my time, energy, money? What does this tell me about my priorities?*
- *Do I have unhealthy habits that pull me away from God?*

For catechumens and candidates, Lent is a time of *purification and enlightenment*, a time to respond to God with greater reflection and commitment.

Body, Mind, and Spirit

The season of Lent speaks to the whole person by appealing not only to the mind and spirit but also to the senses:

Ashes. The ashes we receive on our foreheads on Ash Wednesday remind us of the passage of time and our constant need of repentance. Wearing ashes on our foreheads indicates our willingness to do penance for our sins.

Violet. The color of the clergy's vestments and church decorations during Lent symbolizes repentance, reflection, and conversion.

ADULTS

CCC 571–605

Living Lent

- As you read through the lesson, make sure participants have a clear understanding of words that may be unfamiliar to those just learning about the Catholic faith, such as repentance, penance, abstinence, fasting and almsgiving.

Body, Mind, and Spirit

- If you have access to the various physical symbols of Lent, show them to the participants as you discuss them. You can also ask participants if they've seen other symbols around church during the Lenten season.

Why Forty Days?

- Have participants pick one of the passages suggested in the lesson and determine what the passage tells us about Lent. After participants have had enough time to work on their own, invite participants to share what they've learned. Then discuss the symbolic meaning of the forty days as a group.

  Genesis 7:17–18: The Flood continued for forty days, washing away what was sinful and renewing the earth.

  Exodus 34:27–29: Moses went with the Lord for forty days and nights without eating or drinking to write down the words of the Lord's covenant with Israel.

  Deuteronomy 8:2–3: The Israelites wandered in the wilderness for forty years, undergoing affliction while also being nourished by God. Through these forty years God showed the Israelites that it is through the Lord, not bread alone, that they are nourished.

  Matthew 4:1–4: Jesus is tempted by the devil during his forty-day fast in the desert. We imitate Jesus by undergoing our own forty days of prayer and fasting. The words Jesus speaks in verse 4 also refer back to Deuteronomy 8:2–3 and the Lord's command to the Israelites.

  Acts 1:1–5: Jesus appeared to the apostles for forty days after his resurrection, teaching them about the kingdom of God and announcing to them the coming of the holy Spirit.

- As you discuss the origins of Lent, give participants a brief explanation of how the forty days of Lent are counted. While the season of Lent is itself technically forty-four days, there are only forty days of penance and fasting and fasting to reflect Jesus' fasting in the desert. To arrive at forty days, take the forty-four days of Lent, subtract the six Sundays (which are traditionally not days of fasting), and add Good Friday and Holy Saturday.

- Emphasize that it is not the exact count of days that is important during Lent, but the spirit into which we enter as we celebrate. Emphasize that for catechumens and candidates this Lent is an especially important time of purification and enlightenment.

ENLIGHTENMENT

JOURNEY OF FAITH

Palms. On the Sunday before Easter, *Palm Sunday of the Passion of the Lord*, we carry palm branches in imitation of those who honored Jesus by throwing palm branches in his path as he rode into Jerusalem.

Our experience of Lent begins with ashes and words that call us to repentance. The symbols and practices of Lent assist us on our path of conversion. Lent prepares us to sing "Alleluia" to our risen Lord at Easter.

Why Forty Days?

The number forty has a symbolic meaning in Scripture and occurs in both the Old and New Testaments (see Genesis 7:17–18, Exodus 34:27–29, Deuteronomy 8:2–3, Matthew 4:1–4, Acts 1:1–5).

The Gospels of Matthew, Mark, and Luke tell us that Jesus spent forty days in the desert after his baptism in the Jordan River: "Jesus…was led by the Spirit into the desert for forty days, to be tempted by the devil" (Luke 4:1–2). The story of Jesus' temptation in the desert is always the Gospel reading on the first Sunday of Lent.

Jesus' desert experience reminds us of the Israelites who were freed from slavery in Egypt only to wander in the desert for forty years on their way to the Promised Land. During that time, they were tempted to sin and turned away from God.

Jesus reversed the Israelites' failure to stay faithful to God. When the devil tempted him, Jesus didn't give in. He resisted the devil's temptations, the same temptations the Israelites had faced in the desert.

- What tempts you to turn your heart away from God?

A Penitential Season

More than any other Church season, Lent focuses our attention on our human reality—our weaknesses and failings as well as our potential for doing good. Historically, Lent was a time when people did public penance (prayers or actions that express sorrow for sin) to be reconciled with the Church. At the beginning of Lent, the bishop placed ashes on those seeking forgiveness and gave them a public penance to perform. Then at Easter, they were welcomed back to the Eucharist as fully reconciled members of the Church. Today, most parishes provide additional opportunities for celebrating the sacrament of penance and reconciliation.

> "My sacrifice, O God, is a contrite spirit; a contrite, humbled heart, O God, you will not scorn."
>
> *Psalm 51:19*

Lenten practices that express our repentance are prayer, fasting, and almsgiving.

> "Prayer for the good of the soul. Fasting for the good of the body. Almsgiving for the good of our neighbor."
>
> *Gertrude Mueller Nelson*

Prayer

In a sense, Lent is a desert experience for each of us. It's a time to step away from the world and reflect in prayer. It's important to take time to reflect on how we're living our faith and prepare our hearts to hear God's voice so we may respond to his call. Turning our hearts toward God prepares us to take part in the celebration of Easter.

Lent is a time to refocus and strengthen our prayer efforts. If we've been lazy or inconsistent in prayer, Lent is a good time to commit to making a stronger and more regular effort. We may choose to lengthen the time we spend in prayer, try a different prayer form, read the daily Mass readings, pray the rosary or Way of the Cross, or attend daily Mass. Reading a spiritual book may help lead us to a richer prayer experience. Our improved prayer habits may spill over into the Easter season and beyond.

- How will you increase or improve your time in prayer this Lent?

A Penitential Season

- Emphasize that Lent is a call to conversion through penance. Ask the participants to quietly reflect on the things within their own hearts that they would like to change. Give examples of inner conversions—changes in attitudes, dealing with anger in a healthier way, letting go of bad habits or objects of attachment.

Prayer

- As a group, discuss ways to increase or improve the quality of time spent in prayer. Then offer participants some time to reflect on their own prayer life.

Journey of Faith for Adults, Enlightenment and Mystagogy Leader Guide

Fasting

Fasting for religious purposes is a practice of self-discipline as old as the people of God (see 1 Samuel 7:5–16, 1 Kings 21:25–29, Joel 2:12–13, Acts 13:2–3, Acts 14:23). It's an aid to concentration in prayer and a help in refocusing our attention on God. Like other spiritual disciplines, fasting needs to be done in the right spirit and with an open heart.

The Church teaches that **fasting** (limiting the amount of food we eat) and **abstinence** (doing without certain foods) must be combined with prayer and works of charity and other acts of mercy:

> "Is this not, rather, the fast that I choose: releasing those bound unjustly, untying the thongs of the yoke; Setting free the oppressed, breaking off every yoke? Is it not sharing your bread with the hungry, bringing the afflicted and the homeless into your house; Clothing the naked when you see them, and not turning your back on your own flesh?"
>
> *Isaiah 58:6–7*

All Fridays of Lent are days of *abstinence* for those age fourteen and older. Most people abstain from eating meat, but other meaningful sacrifices may be substituted.

Ash Wednesday and Good Friday are required days of *fasting and abstinence* for those between the ages of eighteen and fifty-nine. When *fasting*, a person is permitted to eat one full meal, as well as two smaller meals that together don't equal a full meal. A person's age, health condition, and degree of physical labor will affect how strictly they're obliged to fast.

> "When you fast, anoint your head and wash your face, so that you may not appear to others to be fasting."
>
> *Matthew 6:17–18*

- What value do you see in fasting and abstaining from meat? How much of a sacrifice will this be for you?
- How might fasting and abstinence make you more conscious of Jesus' suffering and sacrifice for our sins? More conscious of those who regularly do without?

Sacrifice and Almsgiving

Our prayer and fasting should lead to sacrifice and **almsgiving** (money or goods given as charity to the poor) and other acts of mercy.

What Jesus Says About Sacrifice

Jesus requires his disciples to make sacrifices in order to follow him:

- Matthew 19:21: "If you wish to be perfect, go, sell what you have and give to [the] poor, and you will have treasure in heaven."
- Mark 8:34: "Whoever wishes to come after me must deny himself, take up his cross, and follow me."
- Luke 14:27, 33: "Whoever does not carry his own cross and come after me cannot be my disciple.... Everyone of you who does not renounce all his possessions cannot be my disciple."

- What is your cross? Will you carry your cross halfheartedly or wholeheartedly?

Members of the early Christian community in Jerusalem gave up ownership of their goods to support the community:

> "All who believed were together and had all things in common; they would sell their property and possessions and divide them among all according to each one's need."
>
> *Acts 2:44–45*

ENLIGHTENMENT · JOURNEY OF FAITH

- Provide time for participants to mark the specific days of fasting and abstinence on their personal calendars and to respond to the reflection questions in their prayer journal.

Sacrifice and Almsgiving

- Emphasize that sacrifice and almsgiving should be done with a Lenten spirit. While these acts can be a good motivator for spring cleaning or personal improvement, personal gain should not be the motivator for Lenten acts of charity or sacrifice.

- Take some time to reflect as a group on the sidebar "What Jesus Says About Sacrifice." Ask participants to discuss what each of the Scripture verses tells us about the nature of sacrifice. Then give participants time to respond to the reflection question on their own.

- Emphasize that in addition to giving up things for Lent, emphasize the need for positive action or change of attitude. Sometimes positive growth is the more difficult thing to do.

Fasting and Abstinence

- Ensure participants understand the difference between fasting and abstinence. Discuss the difference between fasting and dieting, emphasizing that a fast isn't about appearances but about growing in faith and becoming closer to God through sacrifice.

- If participants are unfamiliar with the practice of fasting, provide further explanation. The law of abstinence prohibits eating meat on Fridays during Lent for those fourteen years of age and over. The law of fasting allows only one full meal a day but does not prohibit taking some food in the morning and evening. Eating between meals is prohibited. Fasting is binding for all between the ages of eighteen and fifty-nine. These regulations are considered a serious obligation for all Catholics. However, those who are ill, pregnant, on medication or special diets for health concerns, or those who must work at extremely physical jobs may be exempt from these regulations. In the United States, all Fridays of Lent are days of abstinence. In both the U.S. and Canada, Ash Wednesday and Good Friday are required days of fasting and abstinence.

Living Lent

JOURNEY OF FAITH | ENLIGHTENMENT

Offering up sacrifices during Lent is a reminder that all of our trials and suffering can be united with the suffering of Jesus and offered up in thanksgiving for his great sacrifice:

"If only we suffer with him so that we may also be glorified with him."

Romans 8:17

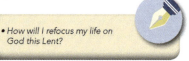
- How will I refocus my life on God this Lent?

When we give something up, our goal is to focus our attention on God and bring him and his concerns back to the center of our lives. Sometimes we discover we need to give something up; other times we may need to do something additional. Through our sacrifices and almsgiving (gifts of charity to the needy), we unite in solidarity with those who regularly do without.

"Giving alms to the poor is a witness to fraternal charity: it is a work of justice pleasing to God."

CCC 2462

"Whoever has two tunics should share with the person who has none. And whoever has food should do likewise."

Luke 3:11

Journey of Faith for Adults: Enlightenment, E2 (826276)
Imprimi Potest: Stephen T. Rehrauer, CSsR, Provincial, Denver Province, the Redemptorists.
Imprimatur: "In accordance with CIC 827, permission to publish has been granted on June 7, 2016, by the Rev. Msgr. Mark Rivituso, Vicar General, Archdiocese of St. Louis. Permission to publish is an indication that nothing contrary to Church teaching is contained in this work. It does not imply any endorsement of the opinions expressed in the publication; nor is any liability assumed by this permission."
Journey of Faith © 1993, 2005, 2016 Liguori Publications, Liguori, MO 63057. To order, visit Liguori.org or call 800-325-9521. Liguori Publications, a nonprofit corporation, is an apostolate of the Redemptorists. To learn more about the Redemptorists, visit Redemptorists.com. All rights reserved. No part of this publication may be reproduced, distributed, stored, transmitted, or posted in any form by any means without prior written permission. Contributing writers: Timothy McCanna and Fr. Richard Thibodeau, CSsR. Editors of 2016 Journey of Faith: Denise Bossert, Julia DiSalvo, and Joan McKamey. Design: Lorena Mitre Jimenez. Images: Shutterstock. Unless noted, Scripture texts in this work are taken from the *New American Bible, revised edition* © 2010, 1991, 1986, 1970 Confraternity of Christian Doctrine, Washington, D.C., and are used by permission of the copyright owner. All Rights Reserved. No part of the *New American Bible* may be reproduced in any form without permission in writing from the copyright owner. Excerpts from English translation of the *Catechism of the Catholic Church* for the United States of America © 1994 United States Catholic Conference, Inc.—Libreria Editrice Vaticana; English translation of the *Catechism of the Catholic Church: Modifications from the Editio Typica* © 1997 United States Catholic Conference, Inc.—Libreria Editrice Vaticana. Compliant with *The Roman Missal, Third Edition*. Printed in the United States of America. 20 19 18 17 16 / 5 4 3 2 1. Third Edition.

Liguori PUBLICATIONS
A Redemptorist Ministry

Journaling

If you have time at the end of the session, have participants respond to the journaling prompt. If not, encourage participants to complete their journal entry at home and use their response as the starting point for their Lenten practices. Encourage participants to explore concrete ways they can grow this Lent. For example, if participants want to become a better example of Christ at home, they should follow up this desire with concrete actions such as taking on housework without complaint, showing more patience to their spouse or children, making time for prayer before family meals, and so on.

Closing Prayer

Ask the participants to close their eyes and silently bring to mind one thing they would like to change about themselves. Then ask the group to pray silently, each person in his or her own way, for the strength and grace needed for this inner conversion. End the session by praying the Glory Be or one decade of the Sorrowful Mysteries.

Looking Ahead

E2: Living Lent is the beginning of the catechumen's journey through Lent. In *E3: Scrutinies*, the participants will go deeper into their preparation for Easter, learning more about the examination of conscience, the causes of guilt, and the God who loves them and wants to forgive, restore, and remake them. As preparation for these lessons, invite participants to reflect on their actions at the end of each day between now and the next session, looking for areas where they can improve on putting Christ first.

E3: Scrutinies: Looking Within

Catechism: 1434–39, 1777–94

Objectives

Participants will…

- Discover that God's mercy is continuously offered freely and to all.
- Define the scrutinies as rites for self-searching and repentance.
- Develop a daily examen of consciousness to begin moving closer to Christ.

Leader Meditation

Matthew 21:28–32

Ask God to forgive the times you intended to do something, but failed to follow through. Spend a moment to look inside yourself and examine your conscience. What keeps you from living your faith as fully as you intend?

Related *Catholic Updates*

- "The Sacrament of Reconciliation: Celebrating God's Forgiveness" (C8603A)
- "Forgiveness in Our Church Today: Key to Healing" (C0304A)

Leader Preparation

- Read the lesson, this lesson plan, the Scripture passage, and the *Catechism* sections.
- Be familiar with the vocabulary term for this lesson: conversion. The definition is provided in this guide's glossary.
- During Lent or prior to their baptism, provide an opportunity for your Christian candidates to receive the sacrament of penance. If this isn't possible, strongly encourage them to go on their own. Also consider scheduling another visit to the church or with the pastor for some Lenten or penitential reflection.

Welcome

Greet participants as they arrive. Check for supplies and immediate needs. Solicit questions or comments about the previous sessions and/or share new information and findings. Begin promptly.

Opening Scripture

Matthew 21:28–32

Light the candle and read the passage out loud. Ask the participants to spend a few moments in silence examining their hearts. When have they let others down by not following through with promises? When have they not lived their faith because they were distracted, embarrassed, or afraid? Emphasize that we, like the first son, can have a change of heart and do what Christ asks of us.

> "The education of the conscience is a lifelong task…The education of the conscience guarantees freedom and engenders peace of heart."
>
> CCC 1784

Journey of Faith for Adults, Enlightenment and Mystagogy Leader Guide

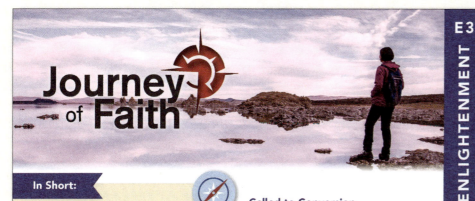

Journey of Faith

E3 ENLIGHTENMENT

In Short:
- God's mercy is continuously offered freely and to all.
- The scrutinies are rites for self-searching and repentance.
- A daily examen of consciousness helps us move closer to Christ.

Scrutinies: Looking Within

We're all familiar with regret. You may regret having that piece of pie at lunch, letting a friendship fade away, or not spending enough time with your family. Though regretful, these actions aren't necessarily sinful.

Most of us will regret *and* feel guilty for the ways we intentionally hurt others and turned away from God through our sinful actions and attitudes. When we sin, we feel the weight of our guilt. We may feel it physically, spiritually, and emotionally. The good news is that we may find ways to express sorrow for the hurt, undo some of the harm we've caused, and get back into right relationship with God, others, and ourselves.

Even better, as we turn back toward God, we discover that God is always turned toward us—with arms outstretched and a heart full of love and mercy, eager to forgive.

- What regrets do you have about hurts you've intentionally caused? How do you feel about yourself as a result?

Called to Conversion

Each test or trial we encounter serves as an opportunity to turn toward, or away from, God. The word **conversion** comes from the Latin for "a turning, overturning, turning around; turning point; change." In spiritual terms, conversion is the ongoing response of our whole person turning in faith and love to the God who loves us.

The first and fundamental conversion occurs at baptism, for "It is by faith in the Gospel and by Baptism that one renounces evil and gains salvation, that is, the forgiveness of all sins and the gift of new life" (CCC 1427).

Many people connect conversion with moral change and the decision to choose right over wrong, good over evil. But morality and law don't save. God saves. Grace saves. The free gift of God's love and mercy makes true morality—choosing to follow God's will out of love, not fear—possible.

"Jesus calls to conversion. This call is an essential part of the proclamation of the kingdom: 'The time is fulfilled, and the kingdom of God is at hand; repent, and believe in the gospel.'"

CCC 1427, citing Mark 1:15

CCC 1434–39; 1777–94

ADULTS

Scrutinies: Looking Within

- As you read through this section, ask participants to share times they've felt regret over something that wasn't a sin. Be prepared to offer some examples of your own. This may also be a good time to emphasize that making a mistake is not the same as committing a sin. For example, miscommunicating something to a coworker isn't the same as intentionally giving them wrong information.

- Discuss as a group the difference between regret and guilt for our actions. Regret may be defined as wishing we'd made a different choice after the fact even though in the moment we thought what we were doing was right. Guilt may be defined as reflecting on a moment where you knew something was wrong at the time, but continued with the action anyway.

- Discuss why it is important to face and trace our guilt and then discuss under what circumstances is guilt a good thing. When is guilt excessive or unhealthy?

Called to Conversion

- Discuss the meaning of conversion given in the lesson. Ask participants how this is the same as or different from a previous definition of conversion they may have learned.

- Discuss with participants why conversion needs to feature both acceptance of God's grace and the personal choice to live a moral life.

What Are the Scrutinies?

- As you read about the scrutinies, emphasize that this rite helps us make sense of the root cause of our guilt and leads us to the peace of wholeness and healing through Christ. process of discernment is called an examination of conscience.

- Reassure participants that the scrutinies are not a test. God does not want us to be stuck in the trap of false guilt, nor does he want us to remain in need of healing. Our creator says, I will remake you, and I loved you even before you asked me to forgive you. This reality should alleviate some anxiety.

- If you have participants who will not be participating in the scrutinies, also discuss the practice of the examination of conscience as a way to understand our feelings of guilt and move away from sin and towards the Lord.

- Discuss how the sacrament of penance can help us face and trace our guilt. Remind candidates that they are welcome and able to receive the sacrament and its benefits, even if they feel some lingering anxiety.

First Scrutiny

- If you have time, read the full story of Jesus and the Samaritan woman (John 4:5–42) out loud. Then give participants time to answer the reflection questions on their own. If you don't have time for the full story, participants can still answer the questions using only the verse, but encourage them to reflect on the whole story on their own.

ENLIGHTENMENT — JOURNEY OF FAITH

What Are the Scrutinies?

When we scrutinize something, we look at it carefully and examine it thoroughly. The rites called the *scrutinies* "are meant to uncover, then heal all that is weak, defective, or sinful in the hearts of the elect; to bring out, then strengthen all that is upright, strong, and good" (*Rite of Christian Initiation of Adults*, 141). The elect look within themselves to find anything that keeps them from Christ. Then they look to Christ to heal those weaknesses and strengthen them when they face temptation.

Three scrutinies for the elect occur on the third, fourth, and fifth Sundays of Lent. (A penitential rite, a type of scrutiny, may be offered for baptized candidates for full communion on or near the second Sunday of Lent.)

Following instruction on the mystery of sin during the catechumenate, the Church invites the elect to reflect on three Gospel stories that reveal the meaning of their upcoming baptism.

First Scrutiny

Christ as Living Water
In the Gospel story of Jesus meeting a Samaritan woman at a well (John 4:5–42), Jesus speaks to her of *living water*:

> "Jesus...said to her, 'Everyone who drinks this water will be thirsty again; but whoever drinks the water I shall give will never thirst; the water I shall give will become in him a spring of water welling up to eternal life.'"
>
> *John 4:13–14*

- How do Jesus' words to the Samaritan woman relate to your upcoming baptism?
- Imagine a spring of water welling up, bubbling up, inside you. What feeling do you connect to this experience?
- How thirsty are you for Christ's living water? What dryness in your life do you hope it will quench?

Second Scrutiny

Christ as the Light of the World
In the Gospel story of Jesus healing a man who was born blind (John 9:1–41), Jesus refers to himself as the *light of the world*:

> "'While I am in the world, I am the light of the world.' When [Jesus] had said this, he spat on the ground and made clay with the saliva, and smeared the clay on [the blind man's] eyes, and said to him, 'Go wash in the Pool of Siloam' (which means Sent). So he went and washed, and came back able to see."
>
> *John 9:5–7*

- When have you been "blind" or unwilling to see the light of Christ? What had your attention or prevented you from seeing?
- Who or what has helped you gain new vision and ability to recognize Christ as the light?
- What blindness (sin) do you want your upcoming baptism to wash away?

Third Scrutiny

Christ as the Resurrection and the Life
In the Gospel story of Jesus raising his friend Lazarus back to life (John 11:1–45), Jesus calls himself the *resurrection and the life*:

> "Jesus said to [Martha], 'Your brother will rise.' Martha said to him, 'I know he will rise, in the resurrection on the last day.' Jesus told her, 'I am the resurrection and the life; whoever believes in me, even if he dies, will live, and everyone who lives and believes in me will never die.'"
>
> *John 11:23–26*

Second Scrutiny

- If you have time, read the full story of Jesus healing the blind man (John 9:1–41) out loud. Then give participants time to answer the reflection questions on their own. If you don't have time for the full story, participants can still answer the questions using only the verse, but encourage them to reflect on the whole story on their own.

Third Scrutiny

- If you have time, read the full story of Jesus raising Lazarus back to life (John 11:1–45) out loud. Then give participants time to answer the reflection questions on their own. If you don't have time for the full story, participants can still answer the questions using only the verse, but encourage them to reflect on the whole story on their own.

Journey of Faith for Adults, Enlightenment and Mystagogy Leader Guide

- The waters of baptism are waters of new life in Christ. What does the promise of salvation, eternal life with God, mean to you?

- How has your life been changing throughout your preparation for baptism?

- How do you expect your life to be different once you have been baptized?

Steps of the Scrutinies

1. After the homily, the elect and their godparents stand before the celebrant.

2. The assembly of the faithful prays in silence, asking that "the elect will be given a spirit of repentance, a sense of sin, and the true freedom of the children of God" (RCIA 152).

3. The celebrant (priest or deacon) invites the elect to pray in silence and may suggest they bow their heads or kneel as "a sign of their inner spirit of repentance" (RCIA 152).

4. He offers prayers of intercession for the elect.

5. He offers a prayer that the elect be "freed from the effects of sin and from the influence of the devil" (RCIA 144).

6. He may lay hands on the head of each of the elect.

7. He makes a final prayer for all the elect with his hands outstretched over them.

8. He either dismisses them to reflect on the Scripture readings or invites them to return to their seats for the Liturgy of the Eucharist.

"The scrutinies are celebrated in order to deliver the elect from the power of sin and Satan, to protect them from temptation, and to give them strength in Christ, who is the way, the truth, and the life. These rites, therefore, should...deepen their resolve to hold fast to Christ and to carry out their decision to love God above all."

RCIA 141

Praying the Examen

Saint Ignatius of Loyola (1491–1556) was a very practical man when it came to prayer. He proposed a daily exercise, which he called the Examen (or Examen of Consciousness), that has been used by many Christians ever since. The Examen is a simple prayer, a prayer for busy people who are continually seeking to do the Lord's will.

There are five simple steps to the Examen, which should take about fifteen minutes to complete:

1. *Recall you are in the presence of God.* In prayer, we place ourselves in God's presence in an especially attentive way. Ask the Holy Spirit to help you look at your life with love this day.

2. *Look at your day with gratitude.* Move through the details of your day in gratitude, remembering that every single event has been God's gift. Take care to notice what you received and what you gave. Thank God for all of these.

3. *Ask help from the Holy Spirit.* Ask for the Holy Spirit to come into your heart and help you look at your actions clearly and with an understanding of your limitations.

4. *Review your day.* Be sure to notice the details, the context of what happened, and how you acted. As you look through the day, notice especially your interior motives and feelings: *When did you fail? When did you love? What patterns and habits do you see? When did you respond positively? Where did you see signs of God's grace in your day?*

5. *Reconcile and resolve.* Talk with Jesus about what you did and what you didn't do. If you failed to love in some way, tell Jesus you're sorry and ask him to be with you the next time the same sort of situation arises. Remember all the good things and thank the Lord for being with you when you avoided a wrong choice or resisted temptation. Feel the sorrow when you apologize, but also feel the gratitude when you give thanks for God's work inside your heart as he labors daily to make you more Christlike.

End the Examen by praying the Our Father.

Steps of the Scrutinies

- Take time to review the steps of the scrutinies given in the lesson. Ask participants if they have any questions about the upcoming rite.

Praying the Examen

- Save time at the end of your session for participants to undergo an Examen on their own. Use the lesson sidebar "Praying the Examen" to get participants started.

Scrutinies: Looking Within

ENLIGHTENMENT

Conversion—our turning to God—happens continuously. We stumble and fall—we sin by failing to keep God first in our lives—but we can get back up and try again thanks to Christ's redeeming love. God eagerly awaits our return, forgives us, and offers us another chance.

- What must die in you so that Christ's new life may take root in you?

Journey of Faith for Adults: Enlightenment, E3 (826276)
Imprimi Potest: Stephen T. Rehrauer, CSsR, Provincial, Denver Province, the Redemptorists.
Imprimatur: "In accordance with CIC 827, permission to publish has been granted on June 7, 2016, by the Rev. Msgr. Mark Rivituso, Vicar General, Archdiocese of St. Louis. Permission to publish is an indication that nothing contrary to Church teaching is contained in this work. It does not imply any endorsement of the opinions expressed in the publication, nor is any liability assumed by this permission."
Journey of Faith © 1993, 2005, 2016 Liguori Publications, Liguori, MO 63057. To order, visit Liguori.org or call 800-325-9521. Liguori Publications, a nonprofit corporation, is an apostolate of the Redemptorists. To learn more about the Redemptorists, visit Redemptorists.com. All rights reserved. No part of this publication may be reproduced, distributed, stored, transmitted, or posted in any form by any means without prior written permission. Contributing writer: Fr. James P. Dunning, PhD. The Examen is taken from the *Catholic Update* "Examen of Consciousness" by Phyllis Zagano. Editors of 2016 *Journey of Faith*: Denise Bossert, Julia DiSalvo, and Joan McKamey. Design: Lorena Mitre Jimenez. Images: Shutterstock. Unless noted, Scripture texts in this work are taken from the *New American Bible, revised edition* © 2010, 1991, 1986, 1970 Confraternity of Christian Doctrine, Washington, D.C., and are used by permission of the copyright owner. All Rights Reserved. No part of the *New American Bible* may be reproduced in any form without permission in writing from the copyright owner. Excerpts from English translation of the *Catechism of the Catholic Church* for the United States of America © 1994 United States Catholic Conference, Inc.—Libreria Editrice Vaticana; English translation of the *Catechism of the Catholic Church: Modifications from the Editio Typica* © 1997 United States Catholic Conference, Inc.—Libreria Editrice Vaticana. *The Rites of the Catholic Church, Volume One* (abbreviated RCIA herein) © 1990 Liturgical Press. Compliant with *The Roman Missal, Third Edition*.
Printed in the United States of America. 20 19 18 17 16 / 5 4 3 2 1. Third Edition.

A Redemptorist Ministry

Journey of Faith for Adults, Enlightenment and Mystagogy Leader Guide

Journaling

It may be advantageous to plan enough time for participants to move directly from their Examen into this journal prompt. However, if you don't have enough time at the end of your session, encourage participants to respond to this prompt on their own time at home, ideally after practicing the Examen again.

Closing Prayer

Invite the class to offer their petitions and to pray this penitential litany:

L: Lord, have mercy.

> R: Lord, have mercy.

L: Christ, have mercy.

> R: Christ, have mercy.

L: Lord, hear us.

> R: Lord, graciously hear us.

L: Lord, guide us as we ponder this week's lesson and sincerely examine our consciences. Send your Holy Spirit to guide us. Help us to feel the tender and affirming touch of the Father's love. You who are love itself, have mercy on us and hear all of our spoken and unspoken petitions. Amen.

Take-Home

During the weeks of the scrutinies or throughout Lent, have participants read and continue to reflect on the three Gospel passages. Remind candidates when they will receive their First Penance or to make an appointment with the pastor.

Scrutinies: Looking Within

E4: The Creed

Catechism: 166–197

Objectives

Participants will...

- Identify the nature and origin of the Creed.
- Describe the meaning of each major belief stated in the Nicene Creed.
- Recognize why a creed is necessary for Church unity and Christian living.

Leader Meditation

The Nicene Creed

Read the Nicene Creed, taking a moment to reflect on the truth expressed in each statement. Prepare to share these reflections, as well as your personal insights and sentiments, during the session.

Related *Catholic Update*

- "The Nicene Creed: What We Believe" (C1205A)

Leader Preparation

- Read the lesson, this lesson plan, the Opening Scripture, and the *Catechism* sections.
- Be familiar with the vocabulary terms for this lesson: consubstantial, begotten, apostolic. Definitions are provided in this guide's glossary.
- Review the prayers for the First Scrutiny and Presentation of the Creed. Gather any special instructions or materials needed to prepare the elect for these rites.
- Part One, Section Two of the *Catechism* (198–1065) works through each phrase of the Nicene Creed in great detail. If specific questions arise, use this resource as a starting point.

Welcome

Check for supplies and immediate needs as each person arrives. After everyone has gathered, welcome the group and give thanks for the unity and support present within it. Solicit questions or comments about previous sessions and/or Catholic beliefs and respond accordingly. Begin promptly.

Opening Scripture

Romans 10:9–11

Light the candle and read the passage aloud. Explain that every time we proclaim the Creed at Mass, we declare our personal *and* shared belief in the Trinity, the Paschal Mystery, and all that stems from them. We confess with our lips what we believe in our hearts and minds.

> "To say the Credo with faith is to enter into communion with God... and also with the whole Church which transmits the faith to us and in whose midst we believe."
>
> CCC 197

Journey of Faith for Adults, Enlightenment and Mystagogy Leader Guide

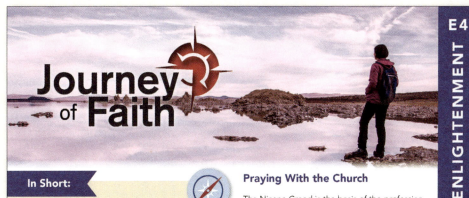

Journey of Faith

ENLIGHTENMENT E4

In Short:
- The Creed is a statement of core beliefs of the faith community.
- The Creed expresses belief in the persons of the Trinity and the Church.
- We are called to share our beliefs and put them into action.

The Creed

Christians believe God is active in our daily lives and loves each of us as if we were his only creation. We also live as a community united in our belief in one God who is Father, Son, and Spirit. As one body—the Church—we join together in faith to read and receive the word, to worship and pray, and to build up the kingdom. We share a way of life, learning to love as Jesus did through the power of the Spirit.

Our communal faith is embodied in the statement of our beliefs: the Creed. After the First Scrutiny, usually during the third week of Lent, you may experience this sense of communal faith in a rite during which you are presented with a copy of the Creed.

Praying With the Church

The Nicene Creed is the basis of the profession of faith new Christians express at their baptism. The words were formulated at the First Council of Nicaea in 325. They summarize our beliefs as passed down, proclaimed, and practiced from the earliest days of the Church. Its principal statements provide an outline of the essential doctrines of the Catholic faith. The Nicene Creed, or the Apostles' Creed on which it's based, is used as the profession of faith of all the faithful at Sunday Mass.

- *Many popular song lyrics and titles include the phrase "I believe." If you wrote a song with that title, how would the lyrics read?*

Breaking It Down

I believe in one God, the Father almighty, maker of heaven and earth, of all things visible and invisible.

Knowing we're loved radically changes our lives. So it is with faith in God. There's a deep hunger within each of us, a space only God can fill. We believe we're created in God's image. When we see the world through God's eyes, we find it "very good" (Genesis 1:31).

What do these passages reveal about God?
- Deuteronomy 26:5–9
- Isaiah 49:15–16
- Jeremiah 31:3
- Luke 15
- Romans 8:38–39

CCC 166–197

ADULTS

The Creed

- Ask participants for examples of modern declarations of shared beliefs and goals, such as mission statements, the Pledge of Allegiance, laws and contracts, etc. Discuss why it's important for groups to have creeds like this, and why it's important all members of these groups have unity in their beliefs.

- Emphasize that the Church greatly values community. In fostering unity and active participation from every member, it fulfills Jesus' prayer for us: "Keep them in your name that you have given me, so that they may be one just as we are" (John 17:11).

Praying With the Church

- Remind participants that the creed is our communal statement of belief as Catholic Christians (see *Q8: Catholic Prayers and Practices*). Remind them that faith is not just about personal beliefs, relationships, or practices.

- Read the Nicene Creed and Apostles' Creed aloud. Ask participants to compare. (These creeds are printed next to each other just before *CCC 185*.) Remind participants that exact wordings, while important, is not as necessary or meaningful as the beliefs and truths behind the words.

- Give participants time to answer the reflection question. If you have time, you might want to share clips of songs feature the phrase "I believe" and ask participants to discuss what the songs have in common and where they differ before creating their own lyrics.

Breaking It Down

- As you discuss each phrase of the Creed, pause to give participants time to complete the three Bible activities in their journal. Allow time to review and share responses as a group (or in small groups) afterward or during the next session. Suggested responses are below:

What do these passages reveal about God?

- Deuteronomy 26:5–9 "The Lord heard our cry and saw our affliction…"
  God saves and redeems his people.

- Isaiah 49:15–16 "I will never forget you."
  God's love is eternal.

- Jeremiah 31:3 "I have loved you; so I have kept my mercy toward you."
  God's mercy is always present and available.

- Luke 15 "What man among you having a hundred sheep and losing one of them would not leave the ninety-nine?"
  God desires the salvation of every person and seeks each one out.

- Romans 8:38–39 "[Nothing] will be able to separate us from the love of God."
  God is greater than time, space, and any earthly creature or power.

The Creed

Allow participants to share personal descriptions or examples of these emotions, and then explore how Jesus handled each of these emotions as our perfect example.

- Tempted: Matthew 4:1–11
  "Jesus was led by the Spirit into the desert to be tempted by the devil."
  In his humanity, Jesus fully experienced our challenges and weaknesses.

- Compassionate: Matthew 9:36
  "His heart was moved with pity for them because they were… like sheep without a shepherd."
  Christ shared the Father's love for humanity.

- Angry: Matthew 21:12–13; Mark 3:5
  "He overturned the tables of the money changers and the seats of those who were selling doves."
  Jesus is fully aware of and opposed to sin and evil in the world.

- Loving: Mark 10:21
  "Jesus, looking at him, loved him and said to him, '…Go, sell what you have, and give to [the] poor and you will have treasure in heaven.'"
  Jesus' commands and preference for the poor come from his love for all, not severity or favoritism.

- Upset: Mark 14:32–42
  "He…began to be troubled and distressed. Then he said to them, 'My soul is sorrowful even to death.'"
  Jesus is impacted by suffering and betrayal.

- Troubled: John 11:33
  "When Jesus saw her weeping…, he became perturbed…"
  Jesus doesn't want anyone to be hurt or suffer.

- Sad: John 11:35–36
  "And Jesus wept."
  Jesus grieves the loss of his loved ones.

ENLIGHTENMENT — JOURNEY OF FAITH

I believe in one Lord Jesus Christ, the Only Begotten Son of God, born of the Father before all ages. God from God, Light from Light, true God from true God, begotten, not made, consubstantial with the Father; through him all things were made. For us men and for our salvation he came down from heaven, and by the Holy Spirit was incarnate of the Virgin Mary, and became man.

These words speak to the mystery of the Trinity. The word **consubstantial** means the Father and the Son are of the same nature and "substance." Christ was **begotten** and possesses the Father's divine nature, just as a child contains his or her biological parents' genetic makeup. Jesus doesn't just tell us about God. He *shows* us God; he *is* God.

God revealed divine love to us in the Son. Miraculously conceived by the Spirit, Jesus was formed in Mary's womb and had a body and soul like ours. While divine, he also shared in our human characteristics and feelings.

These passages describe a feeling or human characteristic of Jesus. *Select one* and reflect on its meaning in your journal.

Jesus was…
tempted: Matthew 4:1–11
compassionate: Matthew 9:36
angry: Matthew 21:12–13; Mark 3:5
loving: Mark 10:21
upset: Mark 14:32–42
troubled: John 11:33
sad: John 11:35–36

For our sake he was crucified under Pontius Pilate, he suffered death and was buried, and rose again on the third day in accordance with the Scriptures. He ascended into heaven and is seated at the right hand of the Father. He will come again in glory to judge the living and the dead and his kingdom will have no end.

God's love is the only power capable of overcoming sin. Jesus invites us to be united with him, turn away from sin, and rise to new life. If Jesus hadn't risen, our faith would be futile and we'd still be enslaved by sin (1 Corinthians 15:17). But Jesus *did* rise. After dying on the cross, he was buried in a sealed and guarded tomb. When women came to anoint his body, the tomb was empty. For forty days, Jesus appeared to his followers, assuring them he had risen.

Jesus passed through death, his human body was transformed into a glorified body, and he will come again in glory. We don't know *how* the world will end. What's important is to be prepared to meet Jesus.

Select an account of Jesus performing a miracle from the list below. Reflect on its message and meaning using the questions that follow.

Healing of a centurion's servant: Matthew 8:5–13
Feeding of the five thousand: Mark 6:34–44
Miraculous catch of fish: Luke 5:1–11
Healing of a paralytic: Luke 5:17–26
Changing water into wine: John 2:1–11
Walking on water: John 6:16–21

Read a passage or two aloud and allow participants to respond to the first two reflection questions. Then give participants time to finish the activity on their own.

- Healing of a centurion's servant: Matthew 8:5–13
  "Jesus said to the centurion, 'You may go; as you have believed, let it be done for you.' And at that very hour [his] servant was healed."
  Jesus rewards the humble and those with faith.

Journey of Faith for Adults, Enlightenment and Mystagogy Leader Guide

- How did the person(s) feel before and after encountering Jesus?
- How might you have felt? What might you have done?
- What areas of your life need healing or liberating?
- How do you expect to feel upon receiving the Easter sacraments?

I believe in the Holy Spirit, the Lord, the giver of life, who proceeds from the Father and the Son, who with the Father and the Son is adored and glorified, who has spoken through the prophets.

Catholics understand the Spirit as the love eternally proceeding from the Father and the Son. The Spirit is the source of our life, the cause of all that's good in the world. We also believe Jesus is the fulfillment of all the Old Covenant laws and words of the prophets.

- How is the Holy Spirit transforming your life?
- How is the Spirit at work in your community, parish, nation, and world?

I believe in one, holy, catholic and apostolic Church. I confess one Baptism for the forgiveness of sins and I look forward to the resurrection of the dead and the life of the world to come. Amen.

The Church is *one*. Christ wants all his followers to be united in him (John 17:21).

The Church is *holy*. We share in the holiness of God through baptism and are called to reject sin and cooperate with the grace of the sacraments.

The Church is *catholic*. This word means "universal" or "whole" and refers to the Christian body throughout the world.

The Church is **apostolic**, tracing its authority and teachings back to Jesus through the apostles. Jesus commissioned them to preach to the world, and we, the Church, are sent every day to share the good news and evangelize.

We confess one Baptism for the forgiveness of sins. In baptism, we die to sin and start a new life in Christ. Baptism removes the corruption of original sin, forgives personal sins, and gives us the strength to overcome temptation (CCC 978).

Our bodies will wear out, but physical death isn't the end. With Jesus, we'll be fully alive in a new world surpassing anything on earth. We don't know how this will happen, but Jesus leaves no doubt about the reality of heaven (John 6:40) and the glory awaiting the faithful.

Amen.

Amen means "yes" or "so be it." We say "yes" to the Father, Son, and Spirit, the promise of eternal life, and the goodness of life in the Church.

ENLIGHTENMENT · JOURNEY OF FAITH

- Walking on water: John 6:16–21
  "They saw Jesus walking on the sea and coming near the boat, and they began to be afraid."
  God commands the forces of nature; nothing prevents him from coming to us.

- Remind participants that because we "confess one Baptism," candidates are already members of the Church, Christ's body, even if they've never professed these particular creeds.

- Identify "one, holy, catholic and apostolic" as the four *marks* (or notes) of the Church and define as needed (see *CCC* 811).

- As you wrap up this lesson, ask participants to think about which creedal statement, belief, or Christian truth inspires them the most and which is the most challenging.

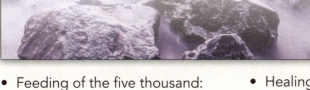

- Feeding of the five thousand: Mark 6:34–44
  "He said the blessing, broke the loaves, and gave them to [his] disciples to set before the people…They all ate and were satisfied. And they picked up twelve wicker baskets full of fragments."
  God's nourishment, particularly in the Eucharist, is abundant, more than sufficient for all.

- Miraculous catch of fish: Luke 5:1–11
  "When they had done this, they caught a great number of fish and their nets were tearing."
  Following Christ in our lives will benefit ourselves as well as many others.

- Healing of a paralytic: Luke 5:17–26
  "I say to you, rise, pick up your stretcher, and go home."
  God heals, forgives our sins, and empowers us to become disciples and witnesses.

- Changing water into wine: John 2:1–11
  "When the headwaiter tasted the water that had become wine…[he] called the bridegroom."
  Christ's words and actions are signs of his divinity, of God's care and blessing, and are done in obedience.

The Creed

- Brainstorm an example or two with the participants before assigning this activity, examples are given in the participant lesson. If you're running out of time in the session, instruct participants to complete the activity at home.

JOURNEY OF FAITH | ENLIGHTENMENT

The Nicene Creed

*I believe in one God,
the Father almighty,
maker of heaven and earth,
of all things visible and invisible.*

*I believe in one Lord Jesus Christ,
the Only Begotten Son of God,
born of the Father before all ages.
God from God, Light from Light,
true God from true God,
begotten, not made, consubstantial with the Father;
through him all things were made.
For us men and for our salvation
he came down from heaven,
and by the Holy Spirit was incarnate of the Virgin Mary,
and became man.
For our sake he was crucified under Pontius Pilate,
he suffered death and was buried,
and rose again on the third day
in accordance with the Scriptures.
He ascended into heaven
and is seated at the right hand of the Father.
He will come again in glory
to judge the living and the dead
and his kingdom will have no end.*

*I believe in the Holy Spirit, the Lord, the giver of life,
who proceeds from the Father and the Son,
who with the Father and the Son is adored and glorified,
who has spoken through the prophets.*

*I believe in one, holy, catholic and apostolic Church.
I confess one Baptism for the forgiveness of sins
and I look forward to the resurrection of the dead
and the life of the world to come. Amen.*

Select several statements from the Creed. Transform each belief into a challenge to action. For example:

- I believe in the Father almighty…so I will obey his commandments.
- I believe in the maker of heaven and earth…so I will care for nature and the environment by…
- I believe the Son rose again on the third day…so I will attend Sunday worship.
- I believe in the resurrection of the dead…so I will visit the cemetery/grave of…

Post them in your home where you'll encounter them regularly.

Journey of Faith for Adults: Enlightenment, E4 (826276)
Imprimi Potest: Stephen T. Rehrauer, CSsR, Provincial, Denver Province, the Redemptorists.
Imprimatur: "In accordance with CIC 827, permission to publish has been granted on June 7, 2016, by the Rev. Msgr. Mark Rivituso, Vicar General, Archdiocese of St. Louis. Permission to publish is an indication that nothing contrary to Church teaching is contained in this work. It does not imply any endorsement of the opinions expressed in the publication, nor is any liability assumed by this permission."
Journey of Faith © 1993, 2005, 2016 Liguori Publications, Liguori, MO 63057. To order, visit Liguori.org or call 800-325-9521. Liguori Publications, a nonprofit corporation, is an apostolate of the Redemptorists. To learn more about the Redemptorists, visit Redemptorists.com. All rights reserved. No part of this publication may be reproduced, distributed, stored, transmitted, or posted in any form by any means without prior written permission. Editors of 2016 Journey of Faith: Denise Bossert, Julia DiSalvo, and Joan McKamey. Design: Lorena Mitre Jimenez. Images: Shutterstock. Text of the Nicene Creed from the English translation of *The Roman Missal, Third Edition* © 2010, International Commission on English in the Liturgy Corporation. Unless noted, Scripture texts in this work are taken from the *New American Bible, revised edition* © 2010, 1991, 1986, 1970 Confraternity of Christian Doctrine, Washington, D.C., and are used by permission of the copyright owner. All Rights Reserved. No part of the New American Bible may be reproduced in any form without permission in writing from the copyright owner. Excerpts from English translation of the *Catechism of the Catholic Church* for the United States of America © 1994 United States Catholic Conference, Inc.—Libreria Editrice Vaticana; English translation of the *Catechism of the Catholic Church: Modifications from the Editio Typica* © 1997 United States Catholic Conference, Inc.—Libreria Editrice Vaticana. *The Rites of the Catholic Church*, Volume One (abbreviated RCIA herein) © 1990 Liturgical Press. Compliant with *The Roman Missal, Third Edition*.
Printed in the United States of America. 20 19 18 17 16 / 5 4 3 2 1. Third Edition.

LIGUORI PUBLICATIONS
A Redemptorist Ministry

Journey of Faith for Adults, Enlightenment and Mystagogy Leader Guide

Closing Prayer

After requesting any special intentions from the group, close with a prayer from the First Scrutiny or Presentation of the Creed.

Looking Ahead

A core message of our faith—and the Creed—is that God sent his only begotten Son to become man, to suffer, die, and rise again for the salvation of all humanity. In preparation for *E5: The Way of the Cross*, ask participants to read a passion account from one of the gospels, taking note of the steps and events along Christ's path. (The Passion narrative can be found in Matthew 15:2–41, Mark 27:11–56, Luke 23:2–49, and John 18:29—19:17–22.)

The Creed

E5: The Way of the Cross

Catechism: 2663–2669

Objectives

Participants will...

- Describe following Jesus as an act that requires both self-denial and sacrifice.
- Identify the Way of the Cross as a prayer that helps us reflect on the cross of Jesus.
- Define the Way of the Cross prayer as fourteen stations marking the path of Jesus' passion and death.

Leader Meditation

Matthew 26–27; Mark 14–15; Luke 22–23; John 18:12—19:38

Slowly and reflectively read any one of the passion accounts. Allow yourself to become part of the crowd, a witness to all that is happening. Let your heart pray in thanksgiving to God for giving us a love so great and complete. Remember that Jesus Christ submitted to his passion and death to open the gates of eternal life that we might come to know the abundant life of Christ.

Related *Catholic Updates*

- "The Way of the Cross: A Lenten Devotion for Our Times" (C8802A)
- "Agony in the Garden: Understanding the Passion of Jesus" (C0802A)

Leader Preparation

- Read the lesson, this lesson plan, the Scripture passage, and the *Catechism* sections.
- If possible, this lesson should take place in church so that the group can move from station to station as each is explained in the lesson. If this isn't possible, try to have images prepared for use in your regular room or encourage participants to walk through the stations at some time during the next few days.
- If you have the resources, purchase a small crucifix for each participant and hand them out as you begin the stations.

Welcome

Greet participants as they arrive. Check for supplies and immediate needs. Solicit questions or comments about the previous sessions and/or share new information and findings. Begin promptly.

Opening Scripture

Mark 15:21–39

Ask for two or more prepared volunteers to light the candle and share the reading. Ask the participants to imagine being witnesses to the suffering and death of Jesus. Have them imagine their feelings and thoughts, and to empathize with the emotions of Jesus' grieving mother and his beloved friends.

> "Christian prayer loves to follow the way of the cross in the Savior's steps. The stations from the Praetorium to Golgotha and the tomb trace the way of Jesus, who by his holy Cross has redeemed the world."
>
> *CCC 2669*

Journey of Faith for Adults, Enlightenment and Mystagogy Leader Guide

Journey of Faith

E5 ENLIGHTENMENT / ADULTS

In Short:
- Following Jesus involves carrying the cross of self-denial and sacrifice.
- The Way of the Cross helps us reflect on the Jesus' cross and our own.
- Traditionally, fourteen stations mark the path of Jesus' passion and death.

The Way of the Cross

Following Jesus involves more than going to Mass every week and being kind to others. To follow Jesus, we must follow the way of the cross.

What does this mean? We learn from Jesus' example that carrying our crosses as his disciples means self-denial and sacrifice. A prayer that helps us enter into this experience is the Way of the Cross (also Stations of the Cross). Fourteen scenes or crosses remind us of the steps Jesus took on his way to his death. We prayerfully walk from station to station and reflect on Christ's passion and death.

> "Whoever wishes to come after me must deny himself, take up his cross, and follow me."
>
> Matthew 16:24

> "Christian prayer loves to follow the way of the cross in the Savior's steps. The stations... trace the way of Jesus, who by his holy Cross has redeemed the world."
>
> CCC 2669

I. Jesus Is Condemned to Death

> "[The crowd] only shouted the louder, 'Crucify him.' So Pilate...released Barabbas to them and, after he had Jesus scourged, handed him over to be crucified."
>
> Mark 15:14–15

Jesus, you faced those who judged and condemned you and felt only love for them. You struggled with fear but continued your mission. You cherished your humanity and your divinity.

Loving Christ, sometimes I lash out to cover my own fears. Show me how to accept myself as a person in the process of growth, painfully struggling to become the person you want me to be. Amen.

II. Jesus Bears His Cross

> "Carrying the cross himself he went out to what is called the Place of the Skull."
>
> John 19:17

Jesus, you willingly accepted your cross. We value power, but you became powerless. We strive for status and control, but you gave yours away. You continued on despite your burden, while we often give up in our daily struggles.

Loving Christ, I often become discouraged with life. I avoid responsibility for my thoughts, feelings, and actions. Teach me to surrender myself, to be generous with my time, talents, and treasures. Amen.

CCC 2663–69

The Way of the Cross

- Before you begin to pray the Way of the Cross with participants, you may want to give some background on the prayer. Emphasize the focus of the Way of the Cross on self-denial and sacrifice, as exemplified in Jesus at his death.

- You may also want to call attention to the stations' foundation in Scripture and Tradition. You may also mention that sometimes a fifteenth station is added to reflect on Jesus' glorious resurrection.

- Encourage participants to visualize themselves carrying their own small crosses and walking in the footsteps of Jesus throughout the prayer. If a group in your parish has provided a small crucifix for each participant, give a crucifix to each catechumen before praying the first station together.

- If you are in church, move the group from station to station. Have willing participants take turns reading the prayers from the lesson that accompany each station. If the church is unavailable, simply read through the lesson together. Consider having a PowerPoint or other visual aid for each station. Try to provide an atmosphere that is solemn, perhaps by dimming lights and asking the participants to minimize talking.

- Encourage questions as this is an "instructional" prayer service. It is not necessary to adhere to the exact format of the lesson.

- Teach participants to pray "We adore you, Oh Christ, and we praise you, for by your holy Cross you have redeemed the world" and help them to know when they are to kneel and recite this prayer.

Handwritten notes:

7 aspects for framework for holiness:

1. patience, perseverance, & meekness
2. Humility
3. Joy/humor
4. Boldness
5. Passion
6. Community
7. Constant prayer

★ Pick one, explain its importance for holiness

★ Which one could you use to help open your eyes like the blind man?

III. Jesus Falls the First Time

Jesus, the burden of the cross was too great. You fell to the dust but pulled yourself up again. Exhausted and suffering, you shouldered your burden while we sometimes force our crosses on others. You continued to move to your destination while we invent excuses to give up our struggles, to abandon our call to follow you.

Loving Christ, I often fail in my struggle to follow you. Show me how to forgive myself. Sometimes I give up hope, lose faith, and refuse to persevere. Your example speaks to me, encouraging me to carry my own cross on my journey back to you. Amen.

IV. Jesus Meets His Mother

Though the Gospels don't record Jesus meeting his mother as he carried the cross, we know she was there at the crucifixion.

Jesus, you showed us we can't shield those we love from pain. You experienced your mother's anguish as she watched you. You gazed with compassion on her pain-filled face.

Loving Christ, teach me to be compassionate to others who are hurting. Teach me to be considerate and loving, as you were to your mother and she was to you. Give me strength to express my feelings of love. Amen.

V. Jesus Is Helped by Simon

"They pressed into service a passer-by, Simon, a Cyrenian... to carry his cross."
Mark 15:21

Jesus, you shared your burden with Simon, showing that we all need help at times.

Loving Christ, inspire me to come forward, step out of the crowd, and acknowledge you. I'm often asked to help, care, or serve, but I refuse. Sometimes I'm offered help, but I don't accept it. Help me say "yes" to helping others and to letting others help me, too. Amen.

VI. Veronica Wipes the Face of Jesus

According to tradition, a woman came forward from the crowd to wipe the sweat and blood from Jesus' face. The likeness of Jesus' face appeared on the veil she used.

Jesus, what courage it must have taken for Veronica to defy the soldiers and offer you comfort!

Loving Christ, at times my faith is weak, and I'm reluctant to be "Christ" for others and to share the message of your salvation. Help me to act and speak in spite of fear or embarrassment. Give me the grace to be more like you, for the sake of others. Amen.

VII. Jesus Falls a Second Time

Jesus, you showed us how to accept human limitations in ourselves and in others. Climbing with your heavy burden, your body gave out once more. You showed us that it's only natural to fail sometimes. You revealed empathy for our struggles to persevere.

Loving Christ, teach me to focus on what you want me to be instead of trying to control others. Help me to stretch out my hand to those who fall and help them up as we journey together in faith, hope, and love. Amen.

VIII. Jesus Speaks to the Women

"Jesus turned to [the women] and said, 'Daughters of Jerusalem, do not weep for me; weep instead for yourselves and for your children.'"

Luke 23:28

Jesus, you told the women to weep over their own oppression. You embraced the powerless and healed the brokenhearted.

Loving Christ, teach me to love mercy and act justly. Help me to appreciate all who touch my life and to bring healing to areas of brokenness wherever I encounter it. Amen.

IX. Jesus Falls a Third Time

Jesus, the burden you carried overpowered you once more, and your body crumpled. With your failing strength, you pulled yourself up again.

Loving Christ, in your weakness you showed me strength. Teach me that it doesn't matter how often I fall along my journey. What counts is that I get up and start again. Help me to trust you to help me become the person I was meant to be. Amen.

X. Jesus Is Stripped of His Garments

"They took his clothes and divided them into four shares, a share for each soldier."

John 19:23

Jesus, you endured the humiliation of being stripped of your clothes. As you stood before the scorn-filled crowd, you gave yourself completely, without reservation.

Loving Christ, teach me to be open and honest in my relationships. Teach me humility. Show me how to become vulnerable because only then will I be able to love. Amen.

XI. Jesus Is Nailed to the Cross

"There they crucified him, and with him two others, one on either side, with Jesus in the middle."

John 19:18

Jesus, you showed us that we will be pierced many times in this life. With each blow of the hammer, the burning metal penetrated deeper into your flesh. You endured the agony of crucifixion for love.

Loving Christ, help me to not crucify others by my words, acts, or omissions. Teach me to let go of negative behavior and transform my vices into virtues. Teach me to build up your body instead of tearing it apart. Amen.

XII. Jesus Dies on the Cross

"Jesus cried out in a loud voice, 'Father, into your hands I commend my spirit'; and...he breathed his last."

Luke 23:46

Jesus, you showed us how to give life and love through your sacrifice. As the weight of your body forced air from your lungs, you thought of us. You asked God to forgive our ignorance and sin.

ENLIGHTENMENT | JOURNEY OF FAITH

The Way of the Cross

- If time permits, add the fifteenth station. If time does not permit you to pray the fifteenth station, use the prayer at the end of this station as the closing prayer for this session.

Optional Fifteenth Station

Jesus Rises From The Dead

After the Sabbath, as the first day of the week was dawning, Mary Magdalene and the other Mary went to see the tomb. And suddenly there was a great earthquake; for an angel of the Lord, descending from heaven, came and rolled back the stone and sat on it. His appearance was like lightning, and his clothing white as snow. For fear of him the guards shook and became like dead men. But the angel said to the women, "Do not be afraid; I know that you are looking for Jesus who was crucified. He is not here; for he has been raised, as he said. Come, see the place where he lay."

Matthew 28:1–6

Prayer: Jesus, you fulfilled your promise and rose from the dead on the third day. The gift of your death and Resurrection makes it possible for us to die and rise. You make it possible for us to become whole and to transform the world. We praise you for the gift of life. Amen.

Loving Christ, you gave everything for me, and I withhold so much. Show me how to live the demands of love more fully so that I might become a true disciple. Help me to understand that by your death you show me how to die and rise each day. Amen.

XIII. Jesus Is Taken From the Cross

"[Joseph] came from the Jewish town of Arimathea and was awaiting the kingdom of God. He went to Pilate and asked for the body of Jesus."

Luke 23:51–52

Jesus, you teach us to trust in you, even when everything seems hopeless. After your death, the few friends near the cross didn't run away even though they were shaken. They reacted courageously and demanded your broken body for burial.

Loving Christ, I am often weak in my faith as I see suffering and death in the world. Teach me that loss and grief can be vehicles of redemption and growth. Help me to transcend the darkness and bring the light of justice, peace, and love to others. Amen.

XIV. Jesus Is Buried in the Tomb

"After [Joseph] had taken [Jesus'] body down, he wrapped it in a linen cloth and laid him in a rock-hewn tomb."

Luke 23:53

Jesus, since it was almost time for Passover, your broken body was hurriedly wrapped in a shroud, rushed to the tomb, and left on a stone slab. Hurrying to bury you before the start of the Jewish Passover, no one took time to clean and anoint your body.

Loving Christ, help me remember the oppressed and forgotten. Help me to not ignore or hurry past those in need. Show me how to love as you have loved me. Amen.

- When have I run from burdens and problems? When have I turned to something other than God as a refuge?
- When have I been tempted to abandon my Lord because of my own frustration or failures?
- Why have I refused to give Jesus my love as completely as he has given his to me?

Journaling

Give participants time to reflect on their experience during the Way of the Cross. Encourage participants to answer all of the journaling prompts in their prayer journal.

This is also a good time to announce what dates or times your parish will be offering the Stations of the Cross during Lent. Encourage participants to join the parish in this devotion and/or to pray it on their own.

Closing Prayer

Use the closing prayer from the fifteenth station.

Looking Ahead

E5: Way of the Cross takes participants through the path our Lord took to gain our redemption and hope for salvation. *E6: The Lord's Prayer* is an in-depth study of the prayer Jesus gave all those who would take up their cross and follow him. Between now and the next session, encourage participants to think about the ways, prayers, and sacraments Jesus gives us as encouragement as we struggle under our own crosses.

E6: The Lord's Prayer

Catechism: 2759–2772

Objectives

Participants will...

- Discover Jesus' invitation to call God, our Father, *Abba*.
- Identify the Lord's Prayer as the prayer Jesus taught his disciples.
- Recall that another name for the Lord's Prayer is the Our Father.

Leader Meditation

Matthew 6:5–15

Examine your own attitudes toward and experiences with prayer. Is prayer a spontaneous part of your life? Do you truly believe God listens to your prayers? How well do you accept God's response when prayers are not answered according to your will? Are you able to hear and see the loving response of God, even when you are feeling disappointed because prayers were not answered exactly as you had hoped?

Related *Catholic Update*

- "Our Father: The Prayer Jesus Taught Us" (C9612A)

Leader Preparation

Read the lesson, this lesson plan, the Scripture passage, and the *Catechism* sections.

Welcome

Greet participants as they arrive. Check for supplies and immediate needs. Solicit questions or comments about the previous sessions and/or share new information and findings. Begin promptly.

Opening Scripture

Matthew 6:5–15

Light the candle and read the passage aloud. Encourage discussion about prayer and God's response to prayer. Ask questions such as: Do you believe that God always answers prayers? How are they answered? How do you feel about seemingly unanswered prayers? Assure the participants that sometimes prayers that we think are unanswered are always heard by God and answered in ways beyond our understanding.

> "When Jesus prays he is already teaching us how to pray. His prayer to his Father is the theological path (the path of faith, hope, and charity) of our prayer to God."
>
> CCC 2607

Journey of Faith for Adults, Enlightenment and Mystagogy Leader Guide

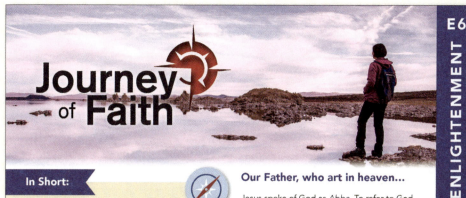

Journey of Faith

E6 ENLIGHTENMENT — ADULTS

In Short:

- Jesus invites us to call God, our Father, our Abba.
- The Lord's Prayer is the prayer Jesus taught his disciples.
- The Lord's Prayer is also known as the Our Father.

The Lord's Prayer

In the Gospels, Jesus provides specific instructions for how to pray. According to Jesus' teaching, the most important aspect is the disposition of our hearts.

> "When you pray, do not be like the hypocrites, who love to stand and pray in the synagogues and on street corners so that others may see them. Amen, I say to you, they have received their reward. But when you pray, go to your inner room, close the door, and pray to your Father in secret. And your Father who sees in secret will repay you."
>
> *Matthew 6:5–6*

During the time of Jesus, the devout Jew prayed in public at set times of the day. Jesus makes the point that we shouldn't pray merely to impress others.

"One of his disciples said to him, 'Lord, teach us to pray'" (Luke 11:1). The Lord's Prayer was Jesus' response to his disciple's request.

In the words Jesus taught us, we pray:

Our Father, who art in heaven...

Jesus spoke of God as *Abba*. To refer to God by the familiar title *Abba* was unheard of in Jewish custom. *Abba* was an intimate name given by children to their father. When Jesus addressed his Father as *Abba*, he was essentially saying "Daddy." By inviting us to call God *Abba*, Jesus reveals to us that we too have a special relationship with God as God's children.

Prayer Suggestions

Imagine God like a loving parent holding you close, telling you how deeply you're loved. As a child rests in the arms of Dad or Mom, relax in the embrace of your loving God.

The psalms tell us why we should praise God. God "is gracious and merciful" and "near to all who call upon him" for help (145:8, 18). God is one who "gives bread to the hungry" (146:7), "healing the brokenhearted, and binding up their wounds" (147:3).

- How have you experienced the qualities of divine love in your life?

Hallowed be thy name; thy kingdom come...

These first petitions reflect our hope and expectation for the kingdom of God to be made fully manifest and present.

> "Go into the whole world and proclaim the gospel to every creature."
>
> *Mark 16:15*

CCC 2759–72

---

participants engaged even as they are opening themselves up to praying the Our Father more deeply and more frequently.

Our Father, who art in heaven...

- Discuss the different images of "father" held by members of the group. Encourage them to view their own fathers—and mothers—as human. Be sensitive to anyone who has or has had a genuinely difficult relationship with a parent, especially a father.

Hallowed be thy name; thy kingdom come...

- Pause here to give participants time to complete the reflection questions.

The Lord's Prayer

- Begin the lesson by reciting the Lord's Prayer together slowly and reverently.

- Discuss good attitudes for prayer with the group. Use the opening reading from Matthew's Gospel for guidelines. If you have participants from other faith traditions, they may mention that this passage from Matthew warns believers not to babble and rely on their many words (some translations use the phrase "mindless repetition" in this passage). It is important to share that the very next thing Jesus does is to entrust to his followers the ultimate prayer. So, rather than being a reason for not praying this prayer, the passage in sacred Scripture calls us to pray this prayer deeply and reverently.

- As you begin, keep in mind the seldom-used words "hallowed" (holy) and "trespasses" (sin, offense, hurt, wounds) may need to be clearly defined.

- In this lesson, there is an opportunity to practice Ignatian prayer (imaginative prayer). Some of your participants may feel more comfortable with this kind of prayer as it is not memorized or ritualized. We have inserted this prayer as a means to keep these

Give us this day our daily bread;

- If you have time, complete the activity as a group. Look up the pope's intentions for the month and offer them up in prayer as a group.

- What specific gift is Jesus inviting you to use in building the kingdom of God? What is your specific mission? Spend time sharing with Jesus your response to his invitation.
- List the names of people who serve God's kingdom in the world today. What do you admire most about them? Thank God for the virtues you see in them. Decide what you can do to become more Christlike in your own attitudes. Pray for the courage to take the first step.

Slowly read the following Scripture passage:

"Do not worry and say, 'What are we to eat?' or 'What are we to drink?' or 'What are we to wear?'... Your heavenly Father knows that you need them all. But seek first the kingdom [of God] and his righteousness, and all these things will be given you besides."

Matthew 6:31–33

Anxiety and worry preoccupy us and drain our energy. They prevent the Spirit of God from freeing us to live the Christian life in a vibrant and victorious way.

- What worries keep you from seeking first the kingdom of God in your life?

Give God each of these worries and ask him to help you set your heart on the kingdom first, knowing that he will care for all the things that trouble or worry you.

Thy will be done on earth as it is in heaven.

Jesus came to reveal the depths of God's boundless love. We pray that, like Jesus, God's will may be done in all we say and do.

Look back over your life. Can you see how your joys, sufferings, and failures are connected to your relationship with God and forming who you are? Can you thank God for the good and beg forgiveness for the bad? Can you say, "For all that has been: I give you thanks, my God! For all that your will holds for me, I give you my full 'yes?'"

- What changes do you need to make in your life to bring it into conformity with God's will? What are the obstacles to doing God's will?
- Think of events that happened to you during the past day, week, and month that really touched your heart and reminded you of God's presence.
- How do these experiences reflect God's will in your life?

Give us this day our daily bread;

According to some biblical scholars, this phrase responds to Jesus calling us to trust him to take care of our needs. Catholics especially profess that Christ himself is our bread of eternal life; he is our "food for the journey."

Prayer Suggestions
Spend some time bringing your needs to God. Picture Christ holding you and your intentions in his heart. As you pray, lift up the needs of the world, the nation, and the Church, as well as your personal intentions.

Christ satisfies our spiritual hunger with the gifts of his Body and Blood in the Eucharist. Receiving holy Communion transforms us into new reflections of the Body of Christ. Jesus is present in the world through our presence to our sisters and brothers.

- How can you make Jesus present in the world through your presence to others?

Did you know that the pope chooses special intentions every month and that the Church is invited to join him in praying for these intentions? Find out what the Holy Father's intentions are for this month.

Forgive us our trespasses as we forgive those who trespass against us;

In this phrase, we acknowledge that we're sinners and also recognize God's great love and mercy. We believe God truly forgives our sins when we seek forgiveness and are willing to forgive the offenses of others. Jesus clearly laid down this latter condition for our forgiveness:

> *"If you forgive others their transgressions, your heavenly Father will forgive you. But if you do not forgive others, neither will your Father forgive your transgressions."*
>
> Matthew 6:14–15

Sometimes, forgiveness is a process that begins with an intention or desire to forgive and only later results in deep healing. Be patient with the process and continue to trust in your ability to forgive through the power of God's merciful love within you.

Contact someone you need to forgive or ask forgiveness from. Invite him or her to meet you for coffee or a meal or to do something you used to enjoy doing together. Keep it light. Ask the Holy Spirit to lead you to a new place in this relationship.

If reaching out to this person is difficult, prepare yourself by:

- Playing some classical or religious music.
- Taking time to relax and quiet yourself.
- Getting in touch with any feelings related to this person or transgression, turning each one over to God.
- Visualizing God as a bright light radiating warmth, compassion, and justice into your heart. Allow the light to expand and surround the person or people affected.
- Asking God to take from you any impediment to reconciliation.
- Taking this person or situation to a trusted confessor or spiritual director.

And lead us not into temptation, but deliver us from evil.

It's easy for us to get lost, fail, or slip into a sudden weakness. When we're empty and aware of our sins, weaknesses, and failures, God can fill, heal, and deliver us.

Prayer Suggestion
Light a candle to represent the light of Christ. Pray that God's power may free you from sinful tendencies. As you pray, imagine the light of God's glory filling the dark areas within you, transforming you into a radiant reflection of God's love to others.

Recite the following prayer over and over, mentioning the areas of weakness (examples: pride, stubbornness, fears, anger, need for control, sexual sins, refusal to trust) from which you most need to be set free:

> *"Come, Lord Jesus, shine the light of our glory on… Oh, Lord, heal and restore me. Set me on my feet again to live the life of grace you had in mind for me when you created me. Amen."*

The peace that Jesus offers his followers is his own peace, which flows from his intimate communion with the Father. It doesn't leave us in times of poverty, suffering, oppression, temptation, or illness. Jesus carries us, lifts us into the arms of our *Abba*, where we encounter the love and peace that surpass all understanding and that sustain us.

- When and how has Jesus lifted you up?

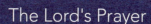

JOURNEY OF FAITH — ENLIGHTENMENT

The Lord's Prayer

Our Father, who art in heaven,
hallowed be thy name;
thy kingdom come;
thy will be done on earth as it is in heaven.
Give us this day our daily bread;
and forgive us our trespasses
as we forgive those who trespass against us;
and lead us not into temptation,
but deliver us from evil.
Amen.

Saint Paul wrote, "No trial has come to you but what is human. God is faithful and will not let you be tried beyond your strength; but with the trial he will also provide a way out, so that you may be able to bear it."

1 Corinthians 10:13

- When have I faced a season of suffering?
- How am I being challenged to trust God now?

Journey of Faith for Adults: Enlightenment, E6 (826276)
Imprimi Potest: Stephen T. Rehrauer, CSsR, Provincial, Denver Province, the Redemptorists.
Imprimatur: "In accordance with CIC 827, permission to publish has been granted on June 7, 2016, by the Rev. Msgr. Mark Rivituso, Vicar General, Archdiocese of St. Louis. Permission to publish is an indication that nothing contrary to Church teaching is contained in this work. It does not imply any endorsement of the opinions expressed in the publication; nor is any liability assumed by this permission."
Journey of Faith © 1993, 2005, 2016 Liguori Publications, Liguori, MO 63057. To order, visit Liguori.org or call 800-325-9521. Liguori Publications, a nonprofit corporation, is an apostolate of the Redemptorists. To learn more about the Redemptorists, visit Redemptorists.com. All rights reserved. No part of this publication may be reproduced, distributed, stored, transmitted, or posted in any form by any means without prior written permission. Contributing writer: Bridget Meehan, SSC. Editors of 2016 Journey of Faith: Denise Bossert, Julia DiSalvo, and Joan McKamey. Design: Lorena Mitre Jimenez. Images: Shutterstock. Unless noted, Scripture texts in this work are taken from the *New American Bible*, revised edition © 2010, 1991, 1986, 1970 Confraternity of Christian Doctrine, Washington, D.C., and are used by permission of the copyright owner. All Rights Reserved. No part of the *New American Bible* may be reproduced in any form without permission in writing from the copyright owner. Excerpts from English translation of the *Catechism of the Catholic Church* for the United States of America © 1994 United States Catholic Conference, Inc.—Libreria Editrice Vaticana, English translation of the *Catechism of the Catholic Church: Modifications from the Editio Typica* © 1997 United States Catholic Conference, Inc.—Libreria Editrice Vaticana. *The Rites of the Catholic Church, Volume One* (abbreviated RCIA herein) © 1990 Liturgical Press. Compliant with *The Roman Missal, Third Edition*. Printed in the United States of America. 20 19 18 17 16 / 5 4 3 2 1. Third Edition.

Liguori PUBLICATIONS
A Redemptorist Ministry

Journey of Faith for Adults, Enlightenment and Mystagogy Leader Guide

Journaling

Allow time at the end of the session for participants to respond to the journal prompt for this lesson. As participants reflect on their own suffering, encourage them to think of God as a father-figure, encouraging them to keep moving forward and drawing them closer to him.

Closing Prayer

Ask the participants to spend several moments in silence, bringing to mind problems, worries, burdens, and special intentions. Ask them to imagine placing these burdens in the arms of the loving and compassionate Father. Close the lesson by asking participants to continue in silent prayer, this time thanking the Father for people, events, and things for which they are most grateful. End with the Sign of the Cross.

Looking Ahead

The previous Lenten lessons have prepared the participants for Holy Week and Triduum. The final Enlightenment lessons will conclude the journey toward Easter and prepare participants for the period of Mystagogy. Encourage participants to reflect on their faith journey so far and write down any especially memorable moments in the prayer journal.

The Lord's Prayer

E7: The Meaning of Holy Week

Catechism: 605–655

Objectives
Participants will…

- Identify Holy Week as a time when we follow the events of Jesus' passion through his resurrection.
- Classify Palm Sunday and the Easter Triduum as the main events of Holy Week.
- Recognize that Jesus entrusts us with sharing the good news of his resurrection with others.

Leader Meditation
A Catechist's Personal Prayer

Me! A spiritual companion for fledgling faith! Loving Spirit of God, I tremble inside. I hold fast to you, great giver of life, offering my prayer of thanksgiving for this very special gift and my prayer of supplication for the graces needed to be worthy of it. Can anything be more important than being a good catechist for one who is about to enter your Church? Overwhelmed by the honor of it, and frightened by the responsibility of it, I say, "Yes, my Lord." It is not clear why you have chosen me, but you clearly have. So I will travel this journey of faith with the ones you have entrusted to my care. We will share our stories, and we will learn more of you as we become a greater Christian witness. Grant us the grace to touch each other's hearts with your tender mercy and your steadfast love. Amen.

Related *Catholic Updates*

- "The Paschal Mystery: God's Wonderful Plan" (C1203A)
- "Lenten Stories From John's Gospel: Baptismal Dramas of Water, Light and Life" (C9603A)
- "Our Holiest Week: A Practical Guide to the Holy Week Liturgies" (C9204A)

Leader Preparation
Read the lesson, this lesson plan, the Scripture passage, and the *Catechism* sections.

Welcome
Greet participants as they arrive. Check for supplies and immediate needs. Solicit questions or comments about the previous sessions and/or share new information and findings. Begin promptly.

Opening Scripture
John 13:1–15

Light the candle and read the passage aloud. Discuss the implications for us today of Jesus' command to wash one another's feet. How do we "wash one another's feet" as we live our daily lives?

> "Therefore Easter is not simply one feast among others, but the 'Feast of feasts,' the 'Solemnity of solemnities.'"
>
> CCC 1169

Journey of Faith for Adults, Enlightenment and Mystagogy Leader Guide

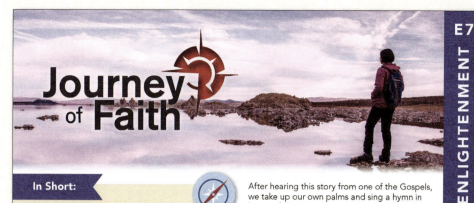

Journey of Faith

ENLIGHTENMENT — E7

In Short:
- During Holy Week, we follow the events of Jesus' passion through his resurrection.
- Palm Sunday and the Easter Triduum mark the main events of Holy Week.
- Jesus entrusts us with sharing the good news of his resurrection with others.

The Meaning of Holy Week

During Holy Week, we enter into Christ's passion, death, and resurrection. We not only commemorate the important events of our salvation in a historical way but we also celebrate them in a sacramental way that makes these sacred mysteries present to us.

Palm Sunday

Holy Week begins on Palm Sunday of the Passion of the Lord, the Sunday before Easter. This liturgy recalls Jesus' dramatic arrival at Jerusalem. He came humbly, yet the people greeted him by laying cloaks and palm branches on his path and acclaiming him as the Son of David, and, therefore, heir to the kingdom.

After hearing this story from one of the Gospels, we take up our own palms and sing a hymn in honor of Christ our king as we process into the church. But the story isn't over. Later, we hear the story of the passion of Jesus. The same people who welcomed Jesus to Jerusalem ask for his crucifixion less than a week later. We reflect on the fickleness of human nature and our own weakness.

A Prayer of Welcoming

Read one of the Gospel accounts of Jesus' triumphal entry into Jerusalem: Matthew 21:1–11, Mark 11:1–10, or Luke 19:28–40.

Now imagine the scene as if you're there. Hear the sounds of the crowd. See the crowd around you, the palms on the path. Watch Jesus riding on the colt of an ass. Imagine you're laying down palms and welcoming Jesus. What else could you do to make Jesus feel honored, respected, and welcomed? We all long to feel welcomed and accepted. When we welcome others, God's welcome to us is passed on.

Remember an opportunity you had recently to welcome someone. It may have been someone who sat next to you in church, someone new at work, someone you just met.

- *What did you do to help this person feel welcomed and accepted?*

ADULTS

CCC 605–655

The Meaning of Holy Week

- Emphasize that Holy Week makes the historical events of the past meaningful and real for us today.
- As you talk about the days of Holy Week, share how your parish celebrates each of these special feasts.

Palm Sunday

- As you discuss Palm Sunday, point out that many Catholics save the palms and present them for burning prior to Ash Wednesday the following year. Last year's palms provided the ashes for this year's Ash Wednesday. This liturgical tradition will appeal to those who like order and are amazed by the significance the Church places on each tradition and how they all fit together.

- Participants may be interested in knowing why palm branches were so important. In biblical times, the palm tree was considered a kingly tree because of its lofty height and majestic appearance, making it a symbol of royalty and victory. The Jewish people carried palm branches in their processions on festive holy days. Roman soldiers carried palms in victory parades. The people of Jerusalem greeted Jesus in the spirit of joy and triumph usually accorded victorious kings and armies. Our palm branches signify a joyful victory, the ultimate victory of Jesus in his Easter triumph over death and sin. The palm branches are a reminder of the victory that awaits each of us as followers of Jesus. While we must endure many sufferings in our own lives, Jesus taught us that this is the way to a victorious resurrection and everlasting life.

A Prayer of Welcoming

- If you have time, divide participants into three groups, one for each of the Gospel accounts given here. Ask groups to read the Gospel account and jot down any details that stand out to them. Then have groups complete the activity.

- When all groups are finished, ask them to share their findings with the other groups.

The Easter Triduum

- As you read about the days of Holy Week, talk specifically about how your parish celebrates these special feasts. Include information about how your parish decorates, chooses music, uses entrance processions, and so on.

- Pause after your discussion of each day's lesson to give participants time to work on the prayer activity.

- Emphasize the great importance of the Holy Saturday celebration and the participants' personal involvement in this holy night. Talk about the meaning of the powerful sacred symbols—light, water, oil, and the cross—that they will see at the Easter Vigil Mass.

- The light shows how the light of Christ dispels our darkness, the water symbolizes how we are cleansed of our sins in baptism, the oil shows we are anointed as followers of Christ, and the cross is the symbol of Christ's glorious death and resurrection.

- Open up the discussion to participants' questions about what will happen during the Easter Vigil Mass, if there are any.

The Easter Triduum

Triduum means a "three-day festival." The Easter Triduum is three days of prayer and worship beginning on Holy Thursday evening and ending with vespers (Evening Prayer) on Easter.

Holy Thursday

Holy Thursday is the feast day of the institution of the priesthood and of the Eucharist.

Chrism Mass. In the morning, in cathedrals around the world, priests and people gather with their bishops for the great chrism Mass. The priests renew their commitment to priestly service, and the people are asked to pray for them.

The three oils used in the Church are blessed by the bishops on Holy Thursday: the *oil of chrism* used in the sacraments of baptism, confirmation, and holy orders; the *oil of catechumens* used in the baptism of children and with adults preparing for baptism; the *oil of the sick* used in the sacrament of the anointing of the sick.

The Mass of the Lord's Supper. The Triduum begins with the evening Mass, which celebrates the institution of the holy Eucharist. After the reading of Jesus' command to serve others as he has served, the celebrant washes the feet of twelve people, representing the twelve apostles whose feet Jesus washed at the Last Supper (see John 13:1–15). At the end of Mass, the priest takes the Blessed Sacrament from the main tabernacle to a separate altar of repose.

Model of Service

Read John 13:1–15. Imagine the scene as if you're there. Imagine Jesus washing your feet: Feel the water on your feet and the towel Jesus uses to dry them. Look at him, bent low in service. He looks up at you and your eyes meet. *How do you feel about Jesus washing your feet?*

Jesus says to you:

"If I, therefore, the master and teacher, have washed your feet, you ought to wash one another's feet. I have given you a model to follow, so that as I have done for you, you should also do."

John 13:14–15

- How is God asking you to "wash feet" in your life?

Good Friday

The central act of worship on this day is the celebration of the passion of the Lord, which has three key parts:

1. *Liturgy of the Word:* We hear the story of the passion from John's Gospel and pray for the Church and the world.

2. *Adoration of the Cross:* We approach the cross with a sign of reverence for this symbol of our salvation, this sign of God's love for us. We reverence the cross because we adore Christ and we thank him for his perfect sacrifice on the cross.

3. *Holy Communion:* Good Friday is the only day in the Church year when Mass isn't offered, but holy Communion reserved from the Mass on Holy Thursday is distributed.

Through Christ's victory over the cross, he offers us everlasting life. During the Good Friday service, the celebrant reminds the assembly three times, "Behold the wood of the Cross, on which hung the salvation of the world" to which we respond, "Come, let us adore."

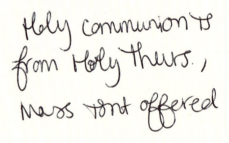

Holy communion from Holy Thurs., Mass not offered

Journey of Faith for Adults, Enlightenment and Mystagogy Leader Guide

A day of abstinence and fasting on which the altar is bare, crosses in the church are covered or removed, and the service ends in silence, Good Friday may be seen by some as dreary and uncomfortable, something to quickly pass over on the way to Easter. But Good Friday can't be skipped over. We must pass through Jesus' death and ponder what it means for us.

At the Foot of the Cross

Imagine standing at the foot of the cross. Take time to visualize Jesus' physical agony. Be aware of your feelings as you witness his sufferings. *What do you want to say to him?*

Listen as Jesus speaks his healing words of forgiveness: "Father, forgive them, they know not what they do" (Luke 23:34). Allow his forgiveness to touch you. Ask Jesus to help you see with his eyes and forgive others as he has forgiven you.

- *Who do you still need to forgive? Picture yourself laying the burden of your anger and hurt at the foot of the cross.*

Holy Saturday

During the day, the Church is silent, the altars are bare. The tabernacle is empty. We wait in silence at the tomb for the Lord's resurrection. We prepare for the Easter sacraments by prayer, reflection, and optional fasting.

After sunset, the Church explodes in joy and celebration of Jesus' resurrection. "This is the night when Christ broke the prison-bars of death," proclaims the Church in the Proclamation of Easter (*Exsultet*). And what a night it is! This is a night when the whole parish and Church come together.

Having attended the Good Friday service, we gather again for the Easter Vigil so that we may experience the complete message of our faith: the assurance that death and sin have been conquered.

The vigil begins at the door of the church where *new fire* is kindled. The priest blesses the new *paschal candle* and lights it from the Easter fire. He or a deacon holds the candle high and carries it into the darkened church, proclaiming "The Light of Christ" to which we respond, "Thanks be to God."

Gradually the light of Christ dispels the darkness. From the paschal candle, other candles are lit until the light fills the church.

The *Liturgy of the Word* leads us to reflect on God's faithful love throughout salvation history. Up to seven *Old Testament readings* are proclaimed, with *psalms* interspersed. We listen to the *epistle* from Romans in which St. Paul writes about our being buried with Jesus Christ "through baptism into death, so that, just as Christ was raised from the dead by the glory of the Father, we too might live in newness of life" (6:4). We sing the "Alleluia" for the first time since Lent began. The *Gospel* and *homily* follow.

Catechumens are called forth for *baptism*. We pray a *Litany of the Saints*. The priest *blesses the water*. Adults and children are baptized, clothed in white garments, and given lighted candles. The assembly renews their baptismal vows.

Candidates for full communion make a *profession of faith*. They join the newly baptized for *confirmation* and later receive the *Eucharist* for the first time.

As with every Mass, we are *sent forth* to be Christ's body in the world. The Mass ends, but the journey of new Catholics has just begun.

Easter

Easter morning follows. New life and fresh hope have come in the risen Christ. We celebrate with a renewal of baptismal promises to reject sin and evil, love God, and follow Jesus.

Easter is such a significant feast that the celebration continues for fifty days. The joyful music, the elegance and fragrance of lilies, and life in Christ, new or renewed, continues until Pentecost...and beyond.

JOURNEY OF FAITH | ENLIGHTENMENT

> Read one of the Gospel accounts of Jesus' resurrection: Matthew 28:1–10; Mark 16:1–8; Luke 24:1–12; or John 20:1–18.
>
> Imagine you're weary and grief-stricken following Jesus' suffering and death. Now you see the empty tomb, the rock that's been rolled away, the wrappings, the angel. Hear the angel announce, "He is not here, for he has been raised just as he said.... Go quickly and tell his disciples" (Matthew 28:6–7).
>
> This message is for us today, too. We are called to be messengers of the good news of Jesus Christ.
>
> - What good news can I share with others about this life of grace and mercy in following the Lord?
>
> - How will I deliver the message in words, in actions, in prayer?

Journey of Faith for Adults: Enlightenment, E7 (826276)
Imprimi Potest: Stephen T. Rehrauer, CSsR, Provincial, Denver Province, the Redemptorists.
Imprimatur: "In accordance with CIC 827, permission to publish has been granted on June 7, 2016, by the Rev. Msgr. Mark Rivituso, Vicar General, Archdiocese of St. Louis. Permission to publish is an indication that nothing contrary to Church teaching is contained in this work. It does not imply any endorsement of the opinions expressed in the publication, nor is any liability assumed by this permission."
Journey of Faith © 1993, 2005, 2016 Liguori Publications, Liguori, MO 63057. To order, visit Liguori.org or call 800-325-9521. Liguori Publications, a nonprofit corporation, is an apostolate of the Redemptorists. To learn more about the Redemptorists, visit Redemptorists.com. All rights reserved. No part of this publication may be reproduced, distributed, stored, transmitted, or posted in any form by any means without prior written permission. Contributing Writers: Fr. Gary Ziuraitis, CSsR, Fr. Bob Rietcheck, CSsR, Fr. Walter Halberstadt, CSsR. Editors of 2016 Journey of Faith: Denise Bossert, Julia DiSalvo, and Joan McKamey. Design: Lorena Mitre Jimenez. Images: Shutterstock. Photo by Denise Bossert. Unless noted, Scripture texts in this work are taken from the *New American Bible*, revised edition © 2010, 1991, 1986, 1970 Confraternity of Christian Doctrine, Washington, D.C., and are used by permission of the copyright owner. All Rights Reserved. No part of the *New American Bible* may be reproduced in any form without permission in writing from the copyright owner. Excerpts from English translation of the *Catechism of the Catholic Church* for the United States of America © 1994 United States Catholic Conference, Inc.—Libreria Editrice Vaticana; English translation of the *Catechism of the Catholic Church: Modifications from the Editio Typica* © 1997 United States Catholic Conference, Inc.—Libreria Editrice Vaticana. *The Rites of the Catholic Church, Volume One* (abbreviated *RCIA* herein) © 1990 Liturgical Press. Compliant with *The Roman Missal*, Third Edition.
Printed in the United States of America. 20 19 18 17 16 / 5 4 3 2 1. Third Edition.

Liguori PUBLICATIONS
A Redemptorist Ministry

Journey of Faith for Adults, Enlightenment and Mystagogy Leader Guide

Journaling

Try to plan time for participants to answer the journal prompt during the session, but give priority to participants' questions about the Easter Vigil Mass.

You may also offer an alternative journal prompt inviting participants to journal about what they are most nervous or most excited about the Easter Vigil Mass. Ask participants to take these things to prayer each day as they get closer to full reception into the Church.

Closing Prayer

As a group, pray:

Good and gracious Lord,

We love you. We praise you. We adore you. You have led each of these dear ones along the faith journey that leads to you, and now we entrust them fully to your rich love and the graces they will receive this week. You are Lord and Creator, the one who formed each life in this room. Shine your love upon them so that they may know you more deeply and more personally than they have ever known. Continue to bless them in the journey.

Amen.

Looking Ahead

The closing prayer for this lesson sets the tone for the final enlightenment lesson during which the participants will experience God's love more deeply and personally in anticipation of their first holy Communion. Ask participants to think about the joy the disciples must have felt at Jesus' resurrection, and then to think about the joy they will feel when they receive Jesus in the Eucharist.

The Meaning of Holy Week

E8: Easter Vigil Retreat

Objectives

Participants will...

- Describe the journey of faith as growing in love of God and his Church.
- Explain how the Easter Vigil Scripture readings help us reflect on our faith journeys.
- Conclude that initiation into the Church as the beginning of full membership and ongoing faith formation.

Leader Meditation

Gather with those leading the retreat, the hospitality team, and your parish priest just prior to the arrival of the candidates and catechumens. Read and reflect on Psalm 92—"It is good to give thanks to the Lord!"

Voice any special intentions, including the success of the Retreat Day. Conclude by praying the Lord's Prayer together or asking for a priestly blessing.

Prepare to welcome the retreatants.

Leader Preparation

- Read the lesson, this lesson plan, and the Scripture passage.
- The end of this retreat is a good time to offer the sacrament of penance and reconciliation. Talk to your parish priest and see if this is a possibility.
- This retreat is based on the Easter Vigil Liturgy of the Word. There are retreat activities for all nine possible readings, but you may not have time for all of them. Find out which readings will be used in your parish for the Easter Vigil, and choose between those activities for the retreat.
- Ideally, the retreat should take place at a retreat center or facility that has an outdoor area where retreatants can walk around safely. If this isn't possible, try to host the retreat somewhere the participants still have room to spread out or walk even if it's all inside.
- Prayer journals (invite participants to bring their own)
- Small pieces of paper and a small fireproof bowl or urn
- One flower for each participant
- Name tags for everyone participating in the retreat (including leaders and the hospitality team)
- Refreshments (snacks, drinks, and food for a light lunch)
- Sponsor and secret intercessor letters for participants (We suggest handing out these leaders after the fourth reading.)
- Bibles

Welcome

Greet participants as they arrive. Alert them to any materials they'll need to start the retreat and encourage them to fill out a nametag.

Opening Prayer

Pray the prayer that appears in the E8 lesson handout together:

Lord, open our minds and hearts to your presence today. Guide us as we journey through this process and bring us closer to you each day. Help us know you better, and help us see your goodness in everyone we meet. Amen.

Journey of Faith

ENLIGHTENMENT / ADULTS — E8

In Short:
- The journey of faith involves growing in love of God and his Church.
- The Scripture readings from the Easter Vigil help us reflect on our faith journeys.
- Initiation into the Church is the beginning of full membership and ongoing formation.

Easter Vigil Retreat

You've come a long way on your journey of faith. You've become part of a faith community, grown in knowledge and awareness of God, and made new friends and memories. You've been preparing for the next step—initiation into the Church and reception of the sacraments.

The reflections and activities during this time of reflection and sharing will help you prepare in heart and spirit for the celebration of Christ's resurrection and the next stage of your faith journey.

Opening Prayer

Lord, open our hearts and minds to your presence. Guide our steps along our journey of faith today and always, so that we may come closer to you every day. Amen.

First Reading: Genesis 1:1—2:2

"God looked at everything he had made, and found it very good."
— Genesis 1:31

Spend some time walking outside by yourself. Become aware of God's presence in creation all around you. When an object or scene catches your eye, ask God what he's trying to reveal to you. For example, a plant growing through a cracked stone or sidewalk might remind you that faith can grow even in tough times. A seedpod may represent the need for patience in your spiritual growth. A sturdy oak may show how faith can grow in strength. Weeds may represent things that distract our focus on God.

If walking outside isn't possible, imagine walking in a park, looking at everything around you until you see something that reminds you of God. When an object or scene catches your eye, ask God what he's trying to reveal to you.

- What do you learn about God from reflecting on his creation of the natural world?

Second Reading: Genesis 22:1–18

"God put Abraham to the test and said to him: Abraham! 'Here I am!' he replied."
— Genesis 22:1

CCC 571–605

Easter Vigil Retreat

First Reading: Genesis 1:1—2:2, activity, and reflection

Follow this reading with a ten-minute talk by a convert from a previous RCIA group. The talk should focus on personal experience, and how grace can become a catalyst for conversion or ongoing conversion. End with a prayer or silent meditation.

Second Reading: Genesis 22:1–18, activity, and reflection

After the reading, have participants answer the reflection questions on a small sheet of paper (let them know they won't have to read their response out loud and that the paper will be disposed of after the activity). Once that's been completed, designate a leader to call out the name of each catechumenate and candidate.

After each person's name is called, the participant should answer, "Here I am!" as Abraham did, come forward, and place his or her piece of paper in the ceramic bowl. After all the names have been called, safely burn the papers. (If you can't safely burn the papers, shred them or dispose of them later.)

Easter Vigil Retreat

Third Reading: Exodus 14:15—15:1 and reflection

Follow the third reading with a ten-minute talk by a convert from a previous RCIA group. The talk should emphasize an experience in which the convert was guided through a difficult time and how God was present during this time. End with a prayer or silent meditation.

Allow time for a short break.

Fourth Reading: Isaiah 54:5–14, activity, and reflection

If you collected letters from participants' sponsors, family members, friends, or secret intercessors distribute those letters now and give participants the opportunity to read and respond to those letters.

If you don't have letters to share with participants, follow the fourth reading with a ten-minute talk by a convert from a previous RCIA group. This talk should emphasize the ways the conversion process made the divine love real for this new Catholic.

Fifth Reading: Isaiah 55:1–11, activity, and reflection

Follow the fifth reading with a ten-minute talk by a convert from a previous RCIA group. This talk should recall a story of discernment and change as RCIA classes ended and the speaker was called to begin a new life in Christ. End with a prayer or silent meditation.

ENLIGHTENMENT — JOURNEY OF FAITH

"Here I am!" Can we respond so eagerly to God's call? God has given Abraham so much, but now God is asking Abraham: *Do you trust me? Are you really ready to answer my call?* As you look forward to entering the Church, these are questions you must answer as well.

- Look back on your faith journey during the RCIA process. What have you felt called to sacrifice or offer during this journey? (A habit that wasn't Christian? A way of thinking? A commitment of time for Mass and RCIA sessions?) It should be a sacrifice that had meaning for you.
- What have you gained as a result of making this sacrifice?

Third Reading: Exodus 14:15—15:1

"Then the LORD said to Moses:...'Lift up your staff and stretch out your hand over the sea, and split it in two, that the Israelites may pass through the sea on dry land.'"

Exodus 14:15–16

God is still working miracles for each of us. As you've gone through the RCIA process, you've traveled on a journey similar to that of the Israelites. God called you from the slavery of sin to the freedom of loving God and others. You've broken with your past life to discover a new life with God and his Church. All along your journey, God has guided and protected you.

- How are you different from when you started the RCIA process?
- What was the most wonderful thing God did for you on this journey? (A special memory? Someone you met? A prayer experience?)
- What has been the most difficult part of the process for you? How has God guided and protected you through that difficult time?

Fourth Reading: Isaiah 54:5–14

"Though the mountains fall away and the hills be shaken, My love shall never fall away from you nor my covenant of peace be shaken, says the LORD, who has mercy on you."

Isaiah 54:10

This is a love letter from God. God is pictured here as a spouse and lover who wants to be reconciled with us, to shower us with love.

A Meditation

Sit in a comfortable position...Close your eyes...Breathe in...Breathe out...Breathe in...Breathe out...Breathe in...Breathe out...Keep paying attention to your breath...If thoughts come, let them go and bring your attention back to your breath.

Now imagine that you're surrounded by God's love just as you're surrounded by the air...With each breath, imagine that you breathe God's love into your whole being...And as you breathe out, you breathe love back to God.

- What human relationship best describes your relationship with God?
- How would your life be different if you believed that God is as close to you as a best friend and cares for you in the same way?

Fifth Reading: Isaiah 55:1–11

"So shall my word be that goes forth from my mouth; It shall not return to me empty, but shall do what pleases me, achieving the end for which I sent it."

Isaiah 55:11

This reading speaks eloquently about the power of God's word.

Journey of Faith for Adults, Enlightenment and Mystagogy Leader Guide

Spend some time in quiet reflection on God's word. Ask God to reveal to you something about your journey through this reading. Read this passage slowly and prayerfully. As you read, be aware of your reactions. What phrase or verse causes the strongest reaction in you? Consider negative reactions as well as positive feelings. A feeling of discomfort or tension might indicate something God wants to show you but that you're resisting.

Silently repeat the phrase that causes strong reaction. Don't think about what it means, simply repeat it over and over. Imagine that you're hearing God repeat the phrase to you. Continue to pray this way for a few minutes.

Now sit silently and reflect on this phrase and how it relates to your life. Talk to God about what thoughts and feelings you have. Listen inside yourself for any response that might be God's prompting.

Finally, let yourself grow silent again and simply sit in the presence of God and God's word.

- What change can you make in your life based on what you've learned from this word of God? Resolve to make this step.

Sixth Reading: Baruch 3:9–15, 32—4:4

"Blessed are we, O Israel; for what pleases God is known to us!"

Baruch 4:4

This reading talks about wisdom. But, as this and other readings make clear, the "wisdom" the world follows isn't always the true wisdom of God. As St. Paul tells us, the wisdom of God often seems foolish to those who look for worldly approval and success. In your journey through the RCIA process, you've learned a lot about the difference between God's perspective and the world's.

Make a list of "wisdom" messages from the world. Then for each piece of the world's "wisdom," write what God's wisdom is, using quotations from Jesus if possible. For example, world wisdom: "Whoever dies with the most toys wins." God's wisdom:

"Do not store up for yourselves treasures on earth, where moth and decay destroy, and thieves break in and steal. But store up treasures in heaven, where neither moth nor decay destroys, nor thieves break in and steal."

Matthew 6:19–20

- What is your definition of wisdom?
- How is it different from what you thought was wise before you joined this group?

Seventh Reading: Ezekiel 36:16–28

"I will give you a new heart, and a new spirit I will put within you. I will remove the heart of stone from your flesh and give you a heart of flesh."

Ezekiel 36:26

A Meditation
Sit in a comfortable position…Close your eyes…Now breathe in…Breathe out…Breathe in…Breathe out…Breathe in…Breathe out…With each breath, imagine that your mind is sinking deeper…deeper to the center of yourself…your heart.

You're still breathing and thinking from your center, your heart…Now ask God to show you your heart…What is it like?…What needs to be changed in your heart?

Now, imagine that God is creating a new heart within you. What is God's heart like?…How do you feel with this new heart within you?

- After the meditation, draw your two hearts, the old and the new, in your journal. In the old heart, write or draw the things that are changing. In the new heart, write or draw what the new heart has that the old heart doesn't.

Sixth Reading: Baruch 3:8–15, 32—44, activity, and reflection

Follow the sixth reading with a ten-minute talk by a convert from a previous RCIA group. This talk should describe how the person's 'wisdom' changed as he or she grew in the Catholic faith. End with a prayer or silent meditation.

Break for lunch.

Seventh Reading: Ezekiel 36:16–28

Follow the seventh reading with a ten-minute talk by a catechumen/candidate from a previous RCIA group. This talk should be a personal witness to the changes that occurred in the convert's heart as he or she grew in the faith.

Meditation

This would be a good opportunity to move the retreat into the parish church (if you're not already there) and offer participants the opportunity to receive the sacrament of penance and reconciliation. If you can, also allow this time for adoration of the Blessed Sacrament as candidates participate in reconciliation. Participants can use the guided meditation in the lesson handout or pray on their own during this time.

Easter Vigil Retreat

Epistle: Romans 6:3–11

When all candidates who wish to receive reconciliation have done so, allow a final moment of silence before reading the epistle.

Gospel:
Matthew 28:1–10 (year A); Mark 16:1–7 (year B); Luke 24:1–12 (year C)

If a priest is available, have the priest read the Gospel from the altar and offer a short homily for the participants on the blessing of Christ's presence in our lives.

Epistle: Romans 6:3–11

"We were indeed buried with him through baptism into death, so that, just as Christ was raised from the dead by the glory of the Father, we too might live in newness of life."

Romans 6:4

- In baptism, we die with Christ. It's natural to be afraid of loss. What fears do you have about changes this step will make in your life?
- In baptism, we're raised with Christ. What hopes do you have about your future in the Church?

Gospel:
Year A, Matthew 28:1–10;
Year B, Mark 16:1–7;
Year C, Luke 24:1–12

"You seek Jesus of Nazareth, the crucified. He has been raised; he is not here."

Mark 16:6

- Reflect on the miracle of Christ's resurrection, Christ's promise to you, and Christ's presence in your life.

Closing Prayer

Lord, you are the resurrection and the life. We have journeyed from darkness to light, from being alone to belonging, from doubt to faith. Guide us on the next step of our journey to make a commitment—a covenant with the living God—Father, Son, and Holy Spirit. Amen.

Journaling

Due to the nature of this lesson, there are no additional activities. Encourage participants to continue writing in their journal throughout the Easter season (mystagogy) and into their lives as Christian adults.

Closing Prayer

The retreat leaders will close their day with the catechumens and candidates using the short prayer found at the end of the E8 lesson handout.

Looking Ahead

Provide the participants with any specific instructions and information they need before the Easter Vigil. Remind them they will enter the final phase (mystagogy) when you reconvene after Easter.

M1: Conversion: A Lifelong Process

Catechism: 160, 545, 981, 1427–29

Objectives

Participants will…

- Identify conversion as a lifelong process.
- Realize both God's grace and our perseverance are needed for spiritual growth.
- Accept that doubts and questions are normal parts of the faith journey.

Leader Meditation

Acts 2:42–47

Consider verses 43 and 45. Two things are at work in the lives of the new believer. He is filled with awe and sensing the call to share with and serve others. This is an excellent description of the period of mystagogy. We are filled with more wonder and awe than we can contain, and that gift of the Holy Spirit fills us so abundantly that it spills over and gives rise to good works for the kingdom of God. God has done this in your life. Now he is doing it in the lives of the neophytes entrusted to your care. Pray for continued outpouring of the Holy Spirit and the manifestation of the gifts each one received at confirmation.

Related *Catholic Updates*

- "The Joy of Being Catholic" (C1405A)
- "Sacraments of Initiation: God's 'I Love You'" (C0904A)
- "Nine Reasons for Going to Mass: Thanksgiving Every Sunday" (C1211A)

Leader Preparation

- Read the lesson, this lesson plan, the Scripture passage, and the *Catechism* sections.
- Collect a few recordings of Easter songs (or those suggested) to use during closing prayer in the weeks to follow. The suggested song for this week is: "How Beautiful," from *Cry for the Desert*, Star Song Music.

Welcome

Greet neophytes as they arrive. Check for supplies and immediate needs. Solicit questions or comments about the previous sessions and/or share new information and findings. Begin promptly.

Opening Scripture

Acts 2:42–47

Light the candle and read the passage aloud. Have the participants imagine they are part of the early Church and witnesses to the spreading of the gospel message. Do they have the same sense of wonder and awe that the first disciples experienced? Are they filled with a desire to serve others and share what they have with those in need? Is the mystery between faith and good works speaking to them in ways they struggle to describe?

> "Christ's call to conversion continues to resound in the lives of Christians. This second conversion is an uninterrupted task for the whole Church."
>
> CCC 1428

Journey of Faith for Adults, Enlightenment and Mystagogy Leader Guide

Journey of Faith

In Short:
- Conversion is a lifelong process.
- God's grace and our perseverance are needed for spiritual growth.
- Having doubts and questions are normal parts of the faith journey.

Conversion: A Lifelong Process

Welcome! You're now a fully initiated member of the Catholic Church.

The Easter Vigil is only the beginning of a commitment to a lifelong discovery and living out of the Christian message. The next stage of the RCIA process is called *mystagogy*, a Greek word meaning "mystery." In the early Church, the community used the fifty days from Easter to Pentecost to explain the mystery of the sacraments celebrated at Easter.

This period is a time for *neophytes* (newly baptized) and those who have come into full communion with the Catholic Church to gain a deeper understanding of God's word, the sacraments, and what your new commitment means for your life. You'll continue to gather for prayer and exploration of Catholic Christianity with a redirected focus—*from learning to living*. You'll be invited to participate more fully in the life of the parish so that your faith may continue to be nourished—and the faith of the community may be enhanced by the witness of its newest members.

- What feelings do you have now that you're a full member of the Catholic Church?

Mountaintops and Valleys

"The soul of one who serves God always swims in joy, always keeps holiday, and is always in the mood for singing."

St. John of the Cross

You may be feeling what St. John of the Cross described. You may also be experiencing other feelings:

- "I felt such a spiritual high during the Easter Vigil. But now everything else seems so... ordinary again."
- "I feel like I've 'graduated.' I guess I don't have to keep coming to these RCIA sessions."
- "I feel kind of confused. I spent so much energy preparing for initiation. Now what do I do?"
- "I really love my new faith but I still have questions. The more I learn, the more I realize I still need to learn."

Peak experiences don't last, even for the apostles. Read about Jesus' transfiguration in Matthew 17:1–9. Peter wanted to stay in this mountaintop experience, but they had to come down from the mountain and get back to the daily grind. Witnessing Jesus' suffering and death caused those special feelings to disappear.

Even though we won't remain in a high state of religious experience all the time, God still walks beside us. When we need to be reassured that God is with us, the Church is there. Prayer, God's word, Mass, the sacraments, our faithful friends—these are all reminders of God's daily presence in our lives.

CCC 160, 545, 981, 1427–29

MYSTAGOGY — ADULTS — M1

Mountaintops and Valleys

- After reading the quotes at the beginning of this section, ask the participants which of the comments in the lesson best describe their own feelings at this time. If they are reluctant to share with the group, offer time for them to respond in their prayer journal.

- Emphasize the existence and importance of mystery in our lives. Talk about the journey that includes mountaintop experiences and the descent that follows.

- Discuss ways to keep some of that mystery as we go about day-to-day living. Encourage participants to use concrete examples.

- We can continue to enter into the mysteries of the sacraments, continue to explore the mysteries of our faith by ongoing faith formation, and experience the mysterious presence of God through our relationships with others and ongoing service in the community.

Conversion: A Lifelong Process

- Give participants time to answer the reflection questions on their own, then discuss as a group. Ask participants how they feel now that they are part of the Church.

- Ask participants how they interpret the difference between *learning* and *living*. If you have time, ask participants for examples of concrete ways they are, or can, live out the faith in their lives.

Ongoing Conversion

- Emphasize that during the process of conversion, there are many highs and lows. Perseverance is key. Periods of doubt are very normal—and are actually an important part of spiritual growth. Conversion is rarely a steady move in the right direction.

- Discuss with participants how their initial conversion may have been different from the ongoing conversion they are now living. Share examples from your own life.

- Provide time for participants to answer the reflection question on their own. Invite volunteers to share their response

Conversion Is Lifelong

- After reading the story of St. Alphonsus Liguori, talk about the meaning of the word *conversion*.

- Discuss with participants why conversion must be a lifelong process and not a single moment of passion or clarity.

MYSTAGOGY — JOURNEY OF FAITH

Ongoing Conversion

The key to this next step is ongoing conversion. At its root, *conversion* means "to change or turn around." Conversion is the ever-present call to grow in faith and to live out that faith. It means deepening our relationship with God and our fellow Christians.

The first step in the conversion process is to turn to Jesus Christ, accept him as our Lord and Savior, and choose to live the life of faith in the community of God's people. This first step, this first turning toward God, is called *initial conversion*. It may be a moving experience, a dramatic moment, one that jars us to the depths of our souls. Or it may happen gradually over a period of years.

Conversion is an ongoing process that requires perseverance and the gradual and continuous redirecting of our lives toward God. Bit by bit, our lives are steered closer to what God wills for us.

Initial conversion needs time, space, and opportunity to sink roots into the rich soil of our lives. Like any living thing, the life of faith requires the right atmosphere to grow and bear fruit. Even Jesus' closest friends and followers grew in their understanding of the Messiah.

The two sons of Zebedee, James and John, asked their mother to intercede for them so that they might sit at Christ's right and left hand in his kingdom:

> "Jesus said in reply, 'You do not know what you are asking. Can you drink the cup that I am going to drink?' They said to him, 'We can.' He replied, 'Whoever wishes to be great among you shall be your servant; whoever wishes to be first among you shall be your slave. Just so, the Son of Man did not come to be served but to serve and to give his life as a ransom for many.'"
>
> *Matthew 20:22, 26–28*

James and John were looking for a warrior king who would rally the people, gather an army, and drive the Romans from their land. Contrary to their expectations, Jesus revealed himself as the "suffering servant" (see Isaiah 53), one who came to serve. As Jesus' apostles, they were being called to this work, and it wasn't what they envisioned.

It was better, fuller!

- *What were your expectations of Jesus and the Church? Did any of these go through changes?*

Conversion Is Lifelong

In the eighteenth century, St. Alphonsus Liguori, an ambitious young Italian lawyer, lost a complicated case. He had been duped, and his whole world collapsed. He stormed out of the courtroom saying, "World, I know you now."

A few weeks later, after a dispute with his domineering father, he walked into a church and heard a voice: "Alphonsus, give yourself to me." He went up the street to the church of Our Lady of Ransom and placed his sword, the symbol of his nobility, on one of the side altars.

This dramatic conversion wasn't the end. Three years later, Alphonsus was ordained a priest. He was vacationing with four other priests on the Amalfi Coast when a sudden storm forced them ashore. They made their way to a mountain hermitage. Overwhelmed by the poverty of the goat herders nearby, Alphonsus dedicated himself to the poor people of the country district. The death of his mentor, Bishop Falcoia, later led Alphonsus to take on the role of leader.

Conversion is a lifelong process. Saint Alphonsus Liguori shows us that. We will each experience many moments of grace and conversion. We'll be changed to the degree we respond to God's grace and our ongoing call to conversion.

- *Describe a recent experience that was a moment of conversion for you. How did you respond to this call to conversion?*

Journey of Faith for Adults, Enlightenment and Mystagogy Leader Guide

All Is Grace

Saint Paul writes: "God is able to make every grace abundant for you, so that in all things, always having all you need, you may have an abundance for every good work."

2 Corinthians 9:8

Saint Thérèse of Lisieux said, "All is grace." If you belong to Jesus Christ, then it's all good. It's all grace.

Grace comes the day we bury a husband or care for an ailing mother. Grace is there when we're raising our children. Grace shows up when we lift our voices and sing our favorite songs. Grace finds us when we care for someone else's children, teach them, and love them. And grace is there when we meet another car at a blind intersection.

Grace is God working in us, through us, and with us so that we can live the life of Christ always and everywhere. It's not a one-time shot in the arm.

Grace is found in the nitty-gritty daily living of the faithful Christian who doesn't give up. It's a gift that flows from baptismal waters into the deepest roots of our souls. It shows up when we need it and to the degree we need it so we can weather any storm.

Anything that draws us closer to God and helps us live out our calling, anything that keeps us close to God...that's grace.

I thought I'd have it all figured out by now...

If you thought you'd have it all figured out by now but don't, welcome to the club! It would be virtually impossible for a thinking, active Catholic to sail through life without questions and doubts. It's part of the faith process. Remember, Jesus didn't dump the apostles because they had doubts or because they couldn't understand everything right away.

Faith is faith precisely because *we do not know, yet still believe*. Recall Jesus' words to Thomas after the resurrection:

> "Have you come to believe because you have seen me? Blessed are those who have not seen and have believed."
>
> *John 20:29*

Faith thrusts us into a lifelong and ongoing relationship with God. Even people engaged in intimate human relationships wonder at times. But a couple can actually grow closer, their love deeper and more mature, after struggling through their doubts. Our doubts can be catalysts to a deeper relationship and closer union with God.

When we face moments of doubt, there are things we can do to remain faithful:

- Get answers from reading Catholic books or from a spiritual director or faithful Catholic.
- Witness to our faith in spite of doubts.
- Intensify our search for understanding through prayer, reading Scripture, and reception of the sacraments.
- Act on our belief and let time and God take care of our doubts.

We can ignore the grace or respond wholeheartedly. God's initiative and invitation aren't what's lacking. We're chased "down the nights and down the days" as described in Francis Thompson's *The Hound of Heaven*.

- When and how have I felt God's pursuit of me? How have I responded?

I thought I'd have it all figured out by now...

- Remind participants that doubts can become catalysts to a deeper relationship or closer union with God. We just have to allow these doubts to send us deeper into our faith journey rather than let them turn us away. Doubts can be unanswered questions or a restless mood. Whatever form they come in for you, embrace them and use them to explore your faith more deeply. There may be times your doubts require you to seek spiritual counseling from a trusted friend or spiritual advisor. Have the courage to reach out.

- As a group, add more examples to the list of ways we can remain faithful in doubt that has been started in the lesson handout.

Conversion: A Lifelong Process

JOURNEY OF FAITH | MYSTAGOGY

Perseverance is the difference between a passing religious experience and the journey of one who, like St. Paul, finishes the course of life well. God's grace and power must begin it all and will continue to lead and sustain us through it all.

- *How do I experience God's grace and power sustaining me on this journey?*

Journey of Faith for Adults: Mystagogy, M1 (826283)
Imprimi Potest: Stephen T. Rehrauer, CSsR, Provincial, Denver Province, the Redemptorists.
Imprimatur: "In accordance with CIC 827, permission to publish has been granted on June 7, 2016, by the Rev. Msgr. Mark S. Rivituso, Vicar General, Archdiocese of St. Louis. Permission to publish is an indication that nothing contrary to Church teaching is contained in this work. It does not imply any endorsement of the opinions expressed in the publication; nor is any liability assumed by this permission."

Journey of Faith for Adults © 2000, 2016 Liguori Publications, Liguori, MO 63057. All rights reserved. No part of this publication may be reproduced, distributed, stored, transmitted, or posted in any form by any means without prior written permission. To order, visit Liguori.org or call 800-325-9521. Liguori Publications, a nonprofit corporation, is an apostolate of the Redemptorists. To learn more about the Redemptorists, visit Redemptorists.com. Contributing Writers: Fr. Jack Murray, CSsR; Fr. Joe Morin, CSsR; Fr. Gary Ziuraitis, CSsR. Editors of 2016 Journey of Faith: Julia DiSalvo, Joan McKamey, and Denise Bossert. Design: Lorena Mitre Jimenez. Images: Shutterstock. Scripture texts in this work are taken from the *New American Bible*, revised edition © 2010, 1991, 1986, 1970 Confraternity of Christian Doctrine, Washington, D.C., and are used by permission of the copyright owner. All Rights Reserved. No part of the *New American Bible* may be reproduced in any form without permission in writing from the copyright owner. Excerpts from English translation of the *Catechism of the Catholic Church* for the United States of America © 1994 United States Catholic Conference, Inc.—Libreria Editrice Vaticana; English translation of the *Catechism of the Catholic Church*: Modifications from the Editio Typica © 1997 United States Catholic Conference, Inc.—Libreria Editrice Vaticana. Compliant with *The Roman Missal, Third Edition.*
Printed in the United States of America 20 19 18 17 16 / 5 4 3 2 1. Third Edition.

LIGUORI PUBLICATIONS
A Redemptorist Ministry

ISBN 978-0-7648-2628-3

Journey of Faith for Adults, Enlightenment and Mystagogy Leader Guide

Journaling

If you have time at the end of the session, invite participants to share their own life experience in response to these questions. If you're out of time, encourage participants to spend time responding to these questions on their own at home.

Closing Prayer

Gather everyone in a circle around the prayer table and listen to the recording of an appropriate song. This week, consider playing "How Beautiful," from *Cry for the Desert*, Star Song Music. (Other suggestions include: "Here I am Lord"; "You Are Mine"; "Shepherd Me, O God"; "One Bread, One Body"; "On Eagle's Wings".)

If music is not available, join hands and pray the Lord's Prayer.

Looking Ahead

In this session you discussed the importance of ongoing and active conversion. In the next session, the neophytes will continue their journey by studying the role of the laity in sharing the gospel message. Between this session and next time, encourage participants to think about what they have to offer their new church community.

Conversion: A Lifelong Process

M2: The Role of the Laity

Catechism: 864, 897–913, 940–43, 1546–47, 2442

Objectives

Participants will...

- Identify the lay (nonordained) faithful as essential to the life of the Church.
- Recognize the laity's call to serve the kingdom of God.
- Describe the laity's call to holiness in the world of family, work, and community.

Leader Meditation

1 Corinthians 12:12–26

Meditate on the reality that you are an indispensable member of the body of Christ. In what ways do you make the body of Christ more whole and more perfect? In what ways are the men and women under your guidance also indispensable members of Christ's body? How does the Church benefit from the great diversity of its membership?

Related *Catholic Updates*

- "The Universal Call to Holiness: Empowering the Laity" (C1209A)
- "From Worship to World: Sent Forth as the Body of Christ" (C1409A)
- "Parish Ministry Today" (C0104A)
- "The Beatitudes: Finding Where Your Treasure Is" (C9112A)

Leader Preparation

- Read the lesson, this lesson plan, the Scripture passage, and the *Catechism* sections.
- Invite your parish director of religious education or other knowledgeable person to attend this session and talk about Church ministries and service opportunities available to parishioners.
- Prepare a map of your city or town and red-capped pins for the activity provided at the end of this lesson (it is not in the participant lesson handout).
- Find a recording of an Easter song to use for the closing prayer. This sessions suggestions include: "Here I am Lord"; "You Are Mine"; "Shepherd Me, O God"; "One Bread, One Body"; "On Eagle's Wings."

Welcome

Greet neophytes as they arrive. Check for supplies and immediate needs. Solicit questions or comments about the previous sessions and/or share new information and findings. Begin promptly.

Opening Scripture

1 Corinthians 12:12–26

Light the candle and read the passage aloud. Ask each person to look at the others in the room. Meditate silently on how every person present has something unique and important to bring to the body of Christ.

> "The very differences which the Lord has willed to put between the members of his body serve its unity and mission. For 'in the Church there is diversity of ministry but unity of mission.'"
>
> CCC 873

Journey of Faith for Adults, Enlightenment and Mystagogy Leader Guide

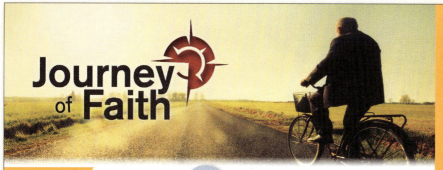

Journey of Faith

M2 MYSTAGOGY

In Short:

- The lay (nonordained) faithful are essential in the life of the Church.
- The laity help serve the kingdom of God.
- Laypeople live out their call to holiness in the world of family, work, and community.

The Role of the Laity

Each of us is tremendously important to God's plan for the world. Drawing on the graces received at baptism, members of the *common priesthood of the faithful* serve God's kingdom. God marks all Christians as children of God, empowering us to act in Christ's name as priests, prophets, and kings.

> "But you are 'a chosen race, a royal priesthood, a holy nation, a people of his own, so that you may announce the praises' of him who called you out of darkness into his wonderful light."
>
> 1 Peter 2:9

As *priests*, laypeople offer worship to God, especially by participating in the eucharistic liturgy. As *prophets*, we speak the word of God and witness to the life, teachings, and saving actions of Christ. As *kings*, we profit from the authority and power of God to continue Christ's ministry of service and love to all people.

The word *layperson* once connoted being a passive recipient of the faith while the ordained priesthood and those in the consecrated life (vowed religious sisters and brothers) were viewed as having an active role in dispensing and passing on the faith. The role of the laity in today's Church is anything but passive.

A layperson is an adopted child of God (Romans 8:15), a sister or brother of Jesus, and an heir to God's wealth of grace and life eternal, called to serve God's kingdom here on earth.

> "While the common priesthood of the faithful is exercised by the unfolding of baptismal grace—a life of faith, hope, and charity, a life according to the Spirit—the ministerial priesthood is at the service of the common priesthood. It is directed at the unfolding of the baptismal grace of all Christians."
>
> CCC 1547

> "No part of the structure of a living body is merely passive but has a share in the functions as well as life of the body: so, too, in the body of Christ, which is the Church."
>
> Decree on the Apostolate of the Laity (*Apostolicam Actuositatem*), 2

- How do you feel called to participate in the Church community?

ADULTS

CCC 864, 897–913, 940–943, 1546–47, 2442

The Role of the Laity

- Read the passage from 1 Peter 2:9 aloud. Discuss with participants what the author means when he refers to us as "a chosen race, a royal priesthood, a holy nation, a people of his own."

- As a group, discuss the ways you see the laity in your parish (or even just the participants in the room) living out the roles of priests, prophets, and kings.

- Discuss with participants the struggles or fears they may face in living out each of their roles in the world.

- Provide time for participants to respond to the reflection question in their prayer journal. Encourage them to find out if your parish offers a ministry through which they can answer their call to participate.

The Role of the Laity

A Shared Work

- Allow time for participants to answer this reflection question in their prayer journal. Emphasize that one's apostolate—or special way of bringing Christ's light to the world—may be very simple and practical.

Doing God's Work in the World

- With the help of the parish director of religious education, talk about opportunities for service and involvement available to laypeople in the parish.

- As a group, create a list of ways participants can do God's work beyond the parish community in their own homes, workplaces, or neighborhoods. Emphasize the different gifts and responsibilities of married couples, parents, single adults, Catholics in the workplace, members of the Church, and Catholic citizens.

A Shared Work

Though the ordained priesthood is unique, bishops, priests, and deacons work in collaboration with the laity. Christ sends the laity into the world to transform the values of society and individuals into those of the kingdom of God, to minister as he would minister.

Before his passion and death, Christ prayed for all his disciples, present and future:

> "They do not belong to the world any more than I belong to the world. Consecrate them in the truth. Your word is truth. As you sent me into the world, so I sent them into the world."
>
> John 17:16–18

Christ identifies his disciples with himself. As a body, we're united with the Father to the same degree the Son is united with the Father and the Holy Spirit in perfect unity.

Each member of Christ's body works in harmony with the rest and is indispensable.

Laypeople go into the world:

> "bearing consistent witness in their personal, family and social lives by proclaiming and sharing the gospel of Christ in every situation in which they find themselves."
>
> On Certain Questions Regarding the Collaboration of the Nonordained Faithful in the Sacred Ministry of the Priest

> "Lay believers are in the front line of Church life; for them the Church is the animating principle of human society. Therefore, they in particular ought to have an ever-clearer consciousness not only of belonging to the Church, but of being the Church."
>
> Pope Pius XII, Discourse, February 20, 1946; see also CCC 899

- How do or can you share the good news of Jesus in the particular circumstances of your life?

Doing God's Work in the World

While we're all called to holiness as a *universal vocation*, we're each also called to a particular vocation. The priesthood of the faithful includes celibate religious, married, and single persons, each with special gifts and opportunities to serve. Each is called to develop the qualities and talents given by God.

> "Love is...the fundamental and innate vocation of every human being.... Christian revelation recognizes two specific ways of realizing the vocation of the human person in its entirety, to love: marriage and virginity or celibacy. Either one is, in its own proper form, an actuation of the most profound truth of man, of his being 'created in the image of God.'"
>
> Pope St. John Paul II, On the Role of the Christian Family in the Modern World (Familiaris Consortio), 11

The whole world is full of opportunities to do God's work. One might consider working in "the more important fields of action, namely, church communities, the family, youth, the social milieu, and national and international levels."

> Decree on the Apostolate of the Laity (Apostolicam Actuositatem), 9

- How are you living out your vocation to love?

As Married Couples and Parents
Husbands and wives are called to help their spouse and children along the path to sainthood. Their primary responsibilities are focused on family life; other kinds of service to the Church come second.

Journey of Faith for Adults, Enlightenment and Mystagogy Leader Guide

"Christian husbands and wives are cooperators in grace and witnesses of faith for each other, their children, and all others in their household. They are the first to communicate the faith to their children and to educate them by word and example for the Christian and apostolic life."

Decree on the Apostolate of the Laity (Apostolicam Actuositatem), 11

As Single Adults

While being single is considered a state of life, not a primary vocation—exclusive and enduring—like marriage, priesthood, and consecrated life, we all share in the fundamental call of Christians to love. Our belonging to God and our call to holiness isn't dependent on marital status.

We find models of Christian living in Scripture. Jesus was single, as were Mary, Martha, Lazarus, and others. Saint Paul saw value in his single status and encouraged others to use their gifts within this state of life:

"Each has a particular gift from God, one of one kind and one of another. Now to the unmarried and to widows I say: it is a good thing for them to remain as they are, as I do."

1 Corinthians 7:7–8

As Workers

Our daily work offers us opportunities to glorify God through the use and development of our talents and our witness to God's love. The ways in which Christian laypersons perform their daily chores can be powerful witnesses to the grace of God.

"In the pilgrimage of this life, [they]... generously dedicate themselves wholly to the advancement of the kingdom of God and to the reform and improvement of the temporal order in a Christian spirit."

Decree on the Apostolate of the Laity (Apostolicam Actuositatem), 4

Sharing Christ in the workplace is a sensitive issue since Christian charity demands we respect the beliefs of others. We don't force Christ on others: Christ *invited* people to believe in him and let the Spirit do the rest. But there will be times when an explicit explanation of the life and work of Jesus Christ may be in order.

In the workplace, there are always opportunities to pray for the needs of fellow workers. Through prayer, God can open hearts to the reception of God's healing.

- *When have you shared your faith at work? How was it received?*

As Church Members

While liturgical ministries such as lector, cantor, and extraordinary minister of holy Communion are important, they're no more important than service to shut-ins, setting up the hall for parish socials, or serving refreshments.

Some laypeople are called to perform tasks that assist priests in serving the needs of the community. Some use their gifts in parish or diocesan administration, pastoral ministry, chaplaincy, bereavement ministry, or faith formation.

"There are innumerable opportunities open to the laity for the exercise of their apostolate of evangelization and sanctification."

Decree on the Apostolate of the Laity (Apostolicam Actuositatem), 6

The Role of the Laity

- Remind participants of the important fact that our primary apostolates are our homes and workplaces. If time allows, complete the "Where Is Our Church?" activity below with your group.

- Display a large map of your town.

- Invite participants to come up and put a pin in their neighborhood, at their workplace, or anywhere else in the community they are actively involved.

- Put a sign above the map, "Where Is Our Church?" and display it in your parish with the invitation for other parishioners to add pins as well.

JOURNEY OF FAITH — MYSTAGOGY

As Community Members and Citizens

Finally, laypersons touch the lives of friends, extended family, and the community in unique and deeply personal ways.

"The effort to infuse a Christian spirit into the mentality, customs, laws, and structures of the community in which one lives is so much the duty and responsibility of the laity that it can never be performed properly by others."

Decree on the Apostolate of the Laity
(Apostolicam Actuositatem), 13

Getting Ready

The laity are most effective as disciples if we're educated and updated in our faith. We can seek out formation opportunities to form us more and more into God's divine image, as a potter forms clay into vessels. Authentic Christian formation takes place within the context of a believing community, usually the local parish, which is centered on the Eucharist, other sacraments, good preaching and teaching, social outreach, and community involvement.

Laypersons may share personal concerns, insights, and inspirations in small groups or seek individual spiritual direction. All adults can grow spiritually through praying regularly, studying Scripture, and reading good books written by respected authors about faith or the spiritual life.

Getting Involved

It's time to take your place alongside other members of the Church community for daily service of the kingdom of God. It's time to get involved and put your faith into action. Some people get involved in Church programs; others bring their faith to secular involvements. Some join groups; others prefer to make a difference as individuals.

- How is God calling me to get involved in my local parish?
- How is God calling me to put my faith into action at work or within the larger community?

Journey of Faith for Adults: Mystagogy, M2 (826283)

Imprimi Potest: Stephen T. Rehrauer, CSsR, Provincial, Denver Province, the Redemptorists.

Imprimatur: "In accordance with CIC 827, permission to publish has been granted on June 7, 2016, by the Rev. Msgr. Mark S. Rivituso, Vicar General, Archdiocese of St. Louis. Permission to publish is an indication that nothing contrary to Church teaching is contained in this work. It does not imply any endorsement of the opinions expressed in the publication, nor is any liability assumed by this permission."

Journey of Faith for Adults © 2000, 2016 Liguori Publications, Liguori, MO 63057. All rights reserved. No part of this publication may be reproduced, distributed, stored, transmitted, or posted in any form by any means without prior written permission. To order, visit Liguori.org or call 800-325-9521. Liguori Publications, a nonprofit corporation, is an apostolate of the Redemptorists. To learn more about the Redemptorists, visit Redemptorists.com. Contributing writer: Fr. Michael Parise. Editors of 2016 Journey of Faith: Julia DiSalvo, Joan McKamey, and Denise Bossert. Design: Lorena Mitre Jimenez. Images: Shutterstock. Scripture texts in this work are taken from the *New American Bible*, revised edition © 2010, 1991, 1986, 1970 Confraternity of Christian Doctrine, Washington, D.C., and are used by permission of the copyright owner. All Rights Reserved. No part of the *New American Bible* may be reproduced in any form without permission in writing from the copyright owner. Excerpts from English translation of the *Catechism of the Catholic Church* for the United States of America © 1994 United States Catholic Conference, Inc.—Libreria Editrice Vaticana; English translation of the *Catechism of the Catholic Church: Modifications from the Editio Typica* © 1997 United States Catholic Conference, Inc.—Libreria Editrice Vaticana. Compliant with *The Roman Missal, Third Edition*.

Printed in the United States of America. 20 19 18 17 16 / 5 4 3 2 1. Third Edition.

Liguori PUBLICATIONS — A Redemptorist Ministry

Journey of Faith for Adults, Enlightenment and Mystagogy Leader Guide

Journaling

As participants respond to these questions, or before you conclude the session, remind neophytes to join a small group in the parish, seek out a spiritual director (priest is a good place to start), and pursue individual study. Encourage them to visit a local Catholic bookstore and browse. Above all, encourage participants to reflect on their unique gifts and opportunities to be Christ to those in the world.

Closing Prayer

At this time, ask the participants to stand in a circle around the prayer table and spend a few moments thanking God for the gift of one another. If music is available, sing along with a recording of an appropriate hymn or song. If music is unavailable, pray the Lord's Prayer.

Looking Ahead

The neophytes have been introduced to the unique call of the laity. Remind them that this calling cannot be fulfilled without the gifts of the Holy Spirit, which they received when they were confirmed, and encourage them to reflect on how receiving the Holy Spirit has impacted their lives and their faith for the next session.

The Role of the Laity

M3: Your Spiritual Gifts

Catechism: 797–810, 2690

Objectives

Participants will…

- Explain how the gifts of the Holy Spirit are manifested in the lives of the faithful.
- Discover how spiritual gifts are to be used in loving service.
- Describe how we can discern, develop, and share our spiritual gifts.

Leader Meditation

1 Corinthians 12:4–11

Saint Paul tells us that, "there are different ministries but the same Lord." Think for a moment about your important ministry as a catechist in the parish RCIA program. What special gifts related to this work has the Spirit given you? Bring them to mind and offer a prayer of thanksgiving to the Holy Spirit for each gift. Know that the Church is grateful for the way you share your gifts.

Related *Catholic Update*

- "Opening the Gifts of the Holy Spirit" (C9802A)

Leader Preparation

- Read the lesson, this lesson plan, the Scripture passage, and the *Catechism* sections.
- Find a recording of an Easter song to use for the closing prayer.

Welcome

- Greet neophytes as they arrive. Check for supplies and immediate needs. Solicit questions or comments about the previous sessions and/or share new information and findings. Begin promptly.

Opening Scripture

1 Corinthians 12:4–11

Light the candle and read the passage aloud. Have each participant consider which gifts mentioned in this passage that they have been given for the building up of the body of Christ by the one Spirit.

> "The Holy Spirit is 'the principle of every vital and truly saving action in each part of the Body.' He works in many ways to build up the whole body in charity."
>
> CCC 798

Journey of Faith for Adults, Enlightenment and Mystagogy Leader Guide

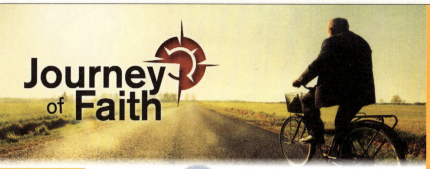

Journey of Faith

MYSTAGOGY — ADULTS — M3

In Short:
- Gifts of the Holy Spirit are manifested in the lives of the faithful.
- All spiritual gifts are to be used in loving service.
- We each must discern, develop, and share our spiritual gifts.

Your Spiritual Gifts

"There are different kinds of spiritual gifts but the same Spirit; there are different forms of service but the same Lord; there are different workings but the same God who produces all of them in everyone. To each individual the manifestation of the Spirit is given for some benefit. To one is given through the Spirit the expression of wisdom; to another the expression of knowledge according to the same Spirit; to another faith by the same Spirit; to another gifts of healing by the one Spirit; to another mighty deeds; to another prophecy; to another discernment of spirits; to another varieties of tongues; to another interpretation of tongues. But one and the same Spirit produces all of these, distributing them individually to each person as he wishes."

1 Corinthians 12:4–11

God has given each Christian two important gifts: the gift of faith in Jesus Christ and the gift of one or more special abilities. These gifts are to be used to unify the body of Christ and to promote the growth of God's kingdom. We receive our spiritual gifts through baptism. As with other gifts, it's impossible to fully appreciate and make use of our spiritual gifts until we've opened them. These gifts are to be used out of love for and in service to one another. We don't choose our gifts; God bestows them on us through the work of the Holy Spirit.

"So that she can fulfill her mission, the Holy Spirit 'bestows upon [the Church] varied hierarchic and charismatic gifts, and in this way directs her.' 'Henceforward the Church, endowed with the gifts of her founder and faithfully observing his precepts of charity, humility and self-denial, receives the mission of proclaiming and establishing among all peoples the Kingdom of Christ and of God, and she is on earth the seed and the beginning of that kingdom.'"

CCC 768, citing Dogmatic Constitution on the Church (Lumen Gentium), 4–5

Let's explore some possible spiritual gifts and consider which ones God has given to us. Once we've discerned our gifts, we'll be better equipped to develop and share them within the Church community and beyond. This sharing of gifts is vital for each individual Christian as well as to the Church as we embrace and carry out our mission of spreading the good news of Jesus Christ.

The Gift of Wisdom

It's said that wisdom comes with age, but it's not automatic. Wisdom is a gift of the Holy Spirit that's attained through having an open mind, learning from experience, knowing human nature, and knowing that God is alive and active in our world. It changes the way we live.

CCC 797–810, 2690

Your Spiritual Gifts

- Following the opening prayer, explain that this lesson focuses on the gifts of the Holy Spirit and their special importance in the lives of the neophytes.
- Ask willing participants to take turns reading about each gift, facilitate discussion and answer questions as needed. After each, give participants time to capture their thoughts and jot down any ministries that interest them.
- Emphasize that we can use these gifts through the simplest of actions. A good example is the gift of healing. A kind and gentle word, in and of itself, can be a source of healing for someone who just needs "a lift."

The Gift of Wisdom

- After reading about the gift of wisdom, discuss the first reflection question as a group, then provide quiet time for participants to respond to the second question on their own.
- Suggested responses include: evangelizing to others, responding to questions about the faith, knowing when it's better not to respond (out of anger or resentment), etc.

The Gift of Knowledge

- After reading about the gift of knowledge, discuss the first reflection question as a group, then provide quiet time for participants to respond to the second question on their own.

- Suggested responses include: all those who teach the faith to others like catechists or spiritual directors, priests require it to preach, etc.

The Gift of Faith

- After reading about the gift of faith, discuss the first reflection question as a group, then provide quiet time for participants to respond to the second question on their own.

- Suggested responses include: leaving home to be a missionary, continuing to search for answers when you have doubts, joining the consecrated or religious life, etc.

The Gift of Healing

- After reading about the gift of healing, discuss the first reflection question as a group, then provide quiet time for participants to respond to the second question on their own.

- Suggested responses include: volunteering to work in a hospital or rehab center, offering encouragement to a distressed friend, making yourself available to a coworker or family member who needs to talk and really listening, spending time with an elderly parent, etc.

JOURNEY OF FAITH | MYSTAGOGY

"But the wisdom from above is first of all pure, then peaceable, gentle, compliant, full of mercy and good fruits, without inconstancy or insincerity."

James 3:17

"Who among you is wise and understanding? Let him show his works by a good life in the humility that comes from wisdom."

James 3:13

Possible Ministries
- Counseling others formally or informally
- Starting a support group for the grieving, the divorced, or others
- Participating in small faith groups

- What other ministries require the gift of wisdom?
- I express the gift of wisdom by…

The Gift of Knowledge

We all have knowledge we can share with others. The important thing isn't how much knowledge we have but how we express it and share it for the benefit of others.

"We have not received the spirit of the world but the Spirit that is from God, so that we may understand the things freely given us by God. And we speak about them not with words taught by human wisdom, but with words taught by the Spirit, describing spiritual realities in spiritual terms."

1 Corinthians 2:12–13

Possible Ministries
- Leading a Bible study group
- Teaching children in parish faith-formation classes
- Teaching adult-literacy classes

- What other ministries use the gift of knowledge?
- I express the gift of knowledge when…

The Gift of Faith

The gift of faith can seem ordinary because it's something we're all supposed to have. But Jesus told us we can move mountains with a true gift of faith:

"If you have faith the size of a mustard seed, you will say to this mountain, 'Move from here to there,' and it will move. Nothing will be impossible for you."

Matthew 17:20

Possible Ministries
- Contributing money to help the parish or community
- Working in a food pantry or homeless shelter
- Participating in a parish prayer group

- What other ministries use the gift of faith?
- I sense the gift of faith when…

The Gift of Healing

When we think of healing, we may think of miracles that defy explanation. But anything we do to lift a depressed spirit, bring a smile, or touch a hurting heart is also healing. When Lazarus, the brother of Mary and Martha had died,

"Many of the Jews had come to Martha and Mary to comfort them about their brother."

John 11:19

Possible Ministries
- Visiting shut-ins
- Transporting those in nursing homes to Mass
- Taking Communion to shut-ins and those in nursing homes

- What other ministries use the gift of healing?
- The Holy Spirit gave me the gift of healing when…

Journey of Faith for Adults, Enlightenment and Mystagogy Leader Guide

The Gift of Working Mighty Deeds

Mighty deeds aren't necessarily big in the eyes of the world. Sometimes small acts done with great love and trust in God are the mightiest of all.

> "[Jesus] noticed a poor widow putting in two small coins. He said, 'I tell you truly, this poor widow put in more than all the rest; for those others have all made offerings from their surplus wealth, but she, from her poverty, has offered her whole livelihood.'"
>
> Luke 21:2–4

Possible Ministries

- Serving refreshments at parish functions
- Cleaning and maintaining the church
- Repairing the homes of the poor or elderly

- What other ministries use the gift of performing mighty deeds for others?
- I demonstrated the gift of mighty deeds when…

The Gift of Prophecy

Prophecy for the Christian isn't foretelling the future. Prophecy is living according to God's values and announcing them in situations where they don't appear to be present.

> "No prophecy ever came through human will; but rather human beings moved by the holy Spirit spoke under the influence of God."
>
> 2 Peter 1:21

Possible Ministries

- Joining a parish social justice group
- Making your parish accessible and welcoming for those with disabilities
- Speaking out when those around you misunderstand or misrepresent the Catholic faith

- What other ministries use the gift of prophecy?
- I experienced the gift of prophecy when…

The Gift of Discernment of Spirits

It's easy to write off hostile or critical people. But discernment of spirits means we see everyone as a child of God with gifts to share. We seek God's perspective and ask ourselves what God would want us to do.

> "Those who are led by the Spirit of God are children of God….You did not receive a spirit of slavery to fall back into fear, but you received a spirit of adoption, through which we cry, 'Abba, Father!'"
>
> Romans 8:14–15

> "Through faith you are all children of God in Christ Jesus."
>
> Galatians 3:26

> "God our savior, who wills everyone to be saved and to come to knowledge of the truth."
>
> 1 Timothy 2:3–4

Possible Ministries

- Serving on the parish council
- Working on parish finances
- Seeking volunteers for projects

- What other ministries use the gift of discernment of spirits?
- I experienced the gift of discernment of spirits when…

The Gift of Working Mighty Deeds

- After reading about the gift of working mighty deeds, discuss the first reflection question as a group, then provide quiet time for participants to respond to the second question on their own.

- Suggested responses include: responding kindly when someone is rude to your, happily doing housework you'd normally resent, volunteering to take on a task at work you'd normally avoid, etc.

The Gift of Prophecy

- After reading about the gift of prophecy, discuss the first reflection question as a group, then provide quiet time for participants to respond to the second question on their own.

- Suggested responses include: speaking out when you see actions that go against the dignity of the person, participating in prolife rallies or marches, vocalizing the Catholic perspective in conversations with friends or coworkers, etc.

The Gift of Discernment of Spirits

- After reading about the gift of discernment of spirits, discuss the first reflection question as a group, then provide quiet time for participants to respond to the second question on their own.

- Suggested responses include: making an effort to get to know people and their interests or talents, taking the time to understanding the perspectives of people we disagree with, etc.

Your Spiritual Gifts

The Gift of Tongues

- After reading about the gift of tongues, discuss the first reflection question as a group, then provide quiet time for participants to respond to the second question on their own.

- Suggested responses include: evangelizing to people where they are in their faith and not talking down to them, voicing compliments instead of just thinking them, etc.

The Gift of Interpreting Tongues

- After reading about the gift of interpreting tongues, discuss the first reflection question as a group, then provide quiet time for participants to respond to the second question on their own.

- Suggested responses include: responding to criticism with compassion, responding to others with empathy, offering to help your family members or friends who seem overwhelmed, etc.

JOURNEY OF FAITH — MYSTAGOGY

The Gift of Tongues

After the Holy Spirit descended at Pentecost, Peter and the other apostles were able to communicate God's good news so that people from every land could understand. The gift of tongues is expressed in the language of love and compassion. We communicate these things when we express our appreciation, admiration, and encouragement to others.

> "And they were all filled with the holy Spirit and began to speak in different tongues, as the Spirit enabled them to proclaim."
>
> Acts 2:4

> "What I say to you in the darkness, speak in the light; what you hear whispered, proclaim on the housetops."
>
> Matthew 10:27

Possible Ministries
- Leading a committee
- Promoting parish events
- Serving as a lector

- What other ministries rely on the gift of good communication?
- I use the gift of communication when…

The Gift of Interpreting Tongues

We must listen for God's voice in everyday life. Jesus said:

> "But blessed are your eyes, because they see, and your ears, because they hear."
>
> Matthew 13:16

> "For God who said, 'Let light shine out of darkness,' has shone in our hearts to bring to light the knowledge of the glory of God on the face of [Jesus] Christ."
>
> 2 Corinthians 4:6

> "You have the anointing that comes from the holy one, and you all have knowledge."
>
> 1 John 2:20

Possible Ministries
- Comforting the grieving
- Welcoming new people in the parish
- Working with alienated Catholics

- What other ministries use the gift of listening?
- I use the gift of listening when…

- How might I use the gifts God has given me for building up the Church?

Journey of Faith for Adults: Mystagogy, M3 (826283)
Imprimi Potest: Stephen T. Rehrauer, CSsR, Provincial, Denver Province, the Redemptorists.
Imprimatur: "In accordance with CIC 827, permission to publish has been granted on June 7, 2016, by the Rev. Msgr. Mark S. Rivituso, Vicar General, Archdiocese of St. Louis. Permission to publish is an indication that nothing contrary to Church teaching is contained in this work. It does not imply any endorsement of the opinions expressed in the publication; nor is any liability assumed by this permission."
Journey of Faith for Adults © 2000, 2016 Liguori Publications, Liguori, MO 63057. All rights reserved. No part of this publication may be reproduced, distributed, stored, transmitted, or posted in any form by any means without prior written permission. To order, visit Liguori.org or call 800-325-9521. Liguori Publications, a nonprofit corporation, is an apostolate of the Redemptorists. To learn more about the Redemptorists, visit Redemptorists.com. Contributing Writer: Denise Bossert. Editors of 2016 Journey of Faith: Julia DiSalvo, Joan McKamey, and Denise Bossert. Design: Lorena Jimenez. Images: Shutterstock. Text: Portions adapted from *Your Faith*, a Redemptorist Pastoral Publication, © 1993 Redemptorist Publications and © 2004 Liguori Publications, *On Baptism* translated by Rev. S. Thelwall, from Ante-Nicene Fathers, Vol. 3, edited by Alexander Roberts, James Donaldson, and A. Cleveland Coxe (Buffalo, NY: Christian Literature Publishing Co., 1885.) Scripture texts in this work are taken from the *New American Bible*, revised edition © 2010, 1991, 1986, 1970 Confraternity of Christian Doctrine, Washington, D.C., and are used by permission of the copyright owner. All Rights Reserved. No part of the *New American Bible* may be reproduced in any form without permission in writing from the copyright owner. Excerpts from English translation of the *Catechism of the Catholic Church* for the United States of America © 1994 United States Catholic Conference, Inc.—Libreria Editrice Vaticana; English translation of the *Catechism of the Catholic Church: Modifications from the Editio Typica* © 1997 United States Catholic Conference, Inc.—Libreria Editrice Vaticana. Compliant with *The Roman Missal, Third Edition*. Printed in the United States of America. 20 19 18 17 16 / 5 4 3 2 1. Third Edition.

Liguori PUBLICATIONS — A Redemptorist Ministry

Journey of Faith for Adults, Enlightenment and Mystagogy Leader Guide

Journaling

As participants complete the journal prompt for this session, encourage them to consider what steps they can take to actively begin participating in a ministry that will make use of their gifts.

Closing Prayer

Ask the participants to stand in a circle around the prayer table and play an appropriate hymn/song. If it is not possible to conclude with music, pray the Lord's Prayer together.

Take-Home

Before the next session, encourage participants to consider the possibility that Jesus may be drawing them to a ministry they have not thought about until today. Ask them to spend time in prayer discerning if our Lord is directing them to this ministry.

M4: Discernment

Catechism: 407, 800, 1776–94

Objectives

Participants will...

- Define discernment as a decision-making process in which we seek God's will.

- Discover St. Ignatius of Loyola's seven-step discernment process.

- Conclude that we must all practice discernment as part of our spiritual growth.

Leader Meditation

Hebrews 13:7–8,17–21

Though St. Paul is confident that he has a good conscience, he realizes that he will also need the guidance of the Holy Spirit through prayer. He is describing the process of discernment. Spend a moment considering the ways you presently make difficult decisions. Do you practice discernment?

Related *Catholic Updates*

- "Liturgy of the Hours: Sharing Your Day With God" (C1312A)

- "Stealing Moments of Quiet: Finding God in Prayer" (C1505A)

- "Examen of Consciousness: Finding God in All Things" (C0303A)

- "Vocations: How Is God Calling Me?" (C0108A)

- "Five Guidelines for Discerning Your Vocation" (C1307A)

Leader Preparation

- Read the lesson, this lesson plan, the Scripture passage, and the *Catechism* sections.

- Collect symbols representing the Holy Spirit to use during the closing prayer.

- Find a recording of an Easter song to use for the closing prayer. Suggested song for this week is "Make Me What You Will" by David Kauffman, from *Surrender*, Good For the Soul Music.

- Be familiar with the vocabulary term for this lesson: discernment. The definition is provided in this guide's glossary.

Welcome

Greet neophytes as they arrive. Check for supplies and immediate needs. Solicit questions or comments about the previous sessions and/or share new information and findings. Begin promptly.

Opening Scripture

Hebrews 13:7–8, 17–21

Light the candle and read the passage aloud. Reflect on and discuss the need for God's input—the power of the Holy Spirit—in our decision making.

"Man is sometimes confronted by situations that make moral judgments less assured and decisions difficult. But he must always seriously seek what is right and good and discern the will of God expressed in divine law. To this purpose, man strives to interpret the date of experience and the signs of the times assisted by the virtue of prudence, by the advice of competent people, and by the help of the Holy Spirit and his gifts."

CCC 1787–1788

Journey of Faith for Adults, Enlightenment and Mystagogy Leader Guide

Journey of Faith

MYSTAGOGY — M4

In Short:

- Discernment is a decision-making process in which we seek God's will.
- Saint Ignatius of Loyola offers a seven-step discernment process.
- We must all practice discernment as part of our growth in the faith journey.

"I will ask the Father, and he will give you another Advocate to be with you always, the Spirit of truth, which the world cannot accept, because it neither sees nor knows it. But you know it, because it remains with you, and will be in you."

John 14:16–17

Discernment

Should I marry Chris? Have I chosen the right career? Should I become a lector or a cantor? When it comes to making decisions, many of us would like to call God and say:

"I don't know what to do right now. If you'd just point the way, that would be great."

- How do you usually make decisions? Do you follow your head or your heart? Do you write down options or ask the advice of others?

Divine guidance *is* available to us. As Christians, we believe the Holy Spirit lives in our hearts, giving us a sense of God's will for our lives. Before he left this world to return to his Father, Jesus promised us the gift of his Spirit. He told his disciples:

The Holy Spirit leads us into the truth and helps us discover and walk God's path for our lives. But the Holy Spirit isn't the only voice that seeks to guide us in life. Many other voices call out to us, seeking to attract us and influence us to walk in a particular direction.

- What other voices influence your decisions?

The decision-making process (often called **discernment**) can be complicated by our lack of self-knowledge, lack of inner freedom, and desire to manipulate God into saying "yes" to what we want. Yet, with the Holy Spirit on our side and a willingness to learn—through reading, talking with mature Christians, and trial-and-error—we'll begin to recognize and discern the voice of God.

No foolproof paths lead us to certainty concerning God's will in a particular situation, but some guidelines can help us grow in our ability to perceive and discern God's will. Saint Ignatius of Loyola offers some in his *Spiritual Exercises*. As we grow in the art and gift of discernment, we'll develop a method that works best for us.

ADULTS

CCC 407, 800, 1776–94

Discernment

- After reading the introduction to the lesson, allow the participants a few moments to respond to the question, "How do you usually make big decisions?" Then discuss how people go about the decision-making process in different ways.

- Ask participants why they think we need both a well-formed conscience and the guidance of the Holy Spirit.

- Suggested responses include: the Holy Spirit gives us a sense for God's will in our lives and keeps us on the path God intended for us, the voice of the Holy Spirit can't be tempted into rationalizing wrong decisions like we sometimes can be.

- Discuss what an "advocate" is, and then ask participants why they think Jesus calls the Holy Spirit our Advocate. Discuss how is the Holy Spirit different from earthly advocates.

- Answer the reflection question as a group.

- Suggested responses include: our parents, friends, coworkers and employers, influential media figures, news stories, politicians, our neighbors, and so on.

Discernment

Seven Steps of Discernment

- Ask participants to take turns reading the "Seven Steps to Discernment." It might make the process seem clearer if you pose a hypothetical moral dilemma and, as a group, apply the seven steps to that problem.

- As you work through each of the steps, emphasize the importance of Step 3: bringing the available options to prayer. This is the step that we most often neglect. Yet, it is through prayer that we open ourselves to the guidance of the Spirit.

An example is included below. You may use this with your group, or make up your own.

1. You are trying to determine if you should quit your job because, after changes in company culture and policy, you are worried it is no longer an ethical place to work.

2. You could stay in the job with the hope that you can influence the future of your company back toward policies you can support, but you're worried that if you stay you'll become numb to these poor choices or begin to accept them as "the way things are now." To gather information you could: discuss the situation with a coworker or manager you trust, but there's always the chance your concern will be misinterpreted or used against you. You could talk to friends outside of your job to see how they've handled similar situations and to get outside perspectives. You could discuss the situation and any moral implications with a priest or spiritual advisor you trust.

MYSTAGOGY — JOURNEY OF FAITH

Seven Steps of Discernment

Here are seven steps that are based on the guidelines of St. Ignatius of Loyola:

1. Determine the question.

We start by clearly stating what we're trying to decide. For example: *Should I change careers? Should I end this relationship? Should I join this ministry in my parish?* Throughout the process, we ask God to reveal his truth and give us the inner freedom to carry it out.

2. Gather information.

We reflect on the advantages and disadvantages of each alternative, being as creative as possible. There may be more options than just quitting or continuing a job or relationship. Perhaps it's possible to continue in a job or relationship but work toward (or even demand) some definite changes.

We write down the pros and cons of each alternative and take into consideration the effect each alternative may have on our relationship with God, family, or others.

We consider how each alternative fits into the rhythm of your life. God sometimes invites us to a task that's completely different from the way things have always been. If that's what God is doing in our life, we need to recognize that our special abilities and life experiences are in some way a preparation for this new calling.

We identify potential obstacles: *What excessive needs, attachments, or compulsions might prevent me from hearing God's word and doing it? To what extent am I attached to an alternative? How free am I to embrace another direction if I believe it's God's will for me?* Recognizing and admitting obstacles to our inner freedom requires honesty, courage, and patience.

- *What needs or attachments might keep you from seeking God's will in this decision?*

We seek out a good counselor. Saint Ignatius tells us that the devil loves secrecy, whereas God blesses openness. The Bible advises us to "seek counsel from every wise person, and do not think lightly of any useful advice" (Tobit 4:18). It's important to seek the input of a wise spiritual director or friend who knows us well.

3. Pray about the options.

The heart of Christian discernment is the act of bringing the available options to prayer and seeing which option gives us the greatest sense of God's presence, peace, and joy.

> *"Take, Lord, and receive all my liberty, my memory, my understanding and my entire will, all that I have and possess. You have given all to me, Lord, I return it. All is yours; do with it what you will. Give me only your love and your grace, that is enough for me."*
>
> *From the Spiritual Exercises of St. Ignatius of Loyola*

As we pray, we consider if we want one option more than the others. If we do, we ask: *How willing am I to let go of that option if it seems God's calling me in another direction?*

Sometimes, we aren't truly free to move in another direction because of attachment to a particular choice. In situations like this, we need to pray for the grace of inner freedom.

True inner freedom means that we're detached enough from every available option to be free to walk down any path God may call us to walk. It may take weeks or months to come to that point of inner freedom. Ideally, we won't choose an option until we're truly detached.

This part of the discernment process is the most important and challenging. It isn't easy to sincerely say, "Thy kingdom come; thy will be done." Having attained a degree of inner freedom through grace, we pray about the various options available, noting our inner reactions and feelings about each.

3. In this instance, it may be easier to stay where you are and hope things get better. That keeps you from any uncomfortable conversations, and you don't have to risk giving up your current employment, which comes with different complications. But what is God calling you to do? How would Jesus respond in this situation?

Journey of Faith for Adults, Enlightenment and Mystagogy Leader Guide

We imagine living out a particular alternative. The option that consistently fills us with the presence of God's peace and joy over a period of time is most likely God's will.

It may surprise us to know that our truest self desires God's will. It's the false, sinful, and unredeemed self that doesn't believe God's will leads to true freedom and happiness.

Saint Ignatius suggests we consider these questions:

- What advice would you give to another person faced with this same situation?
- Imagine yourself on your deathbed looking back over your life. What do you wish you had chosen in each situation?
- Picture yourself standing before God at the Final Judgment and consider what decision you would then wish to have made.

4. Make a decision.

At some point, we need to make a decision. We go with the option that gives us the most peace in prayer.

If we experience no real peace about the options, we may either postpone the decision or choose the least troublesome option. We shouldn't decide when in doubt, and, if time permits, we continue to pray until we experience peace.

We're aware that the option chosen may not always be the most attractive one or the one we most desired. Sometimes we may feel led to choose an option with tears—for example, to return to a marriage situation that in the past caused much pain. Such initial tears of sadness, however, often give way to tears of joy.

5. Live with the decision.

Once we come to a decision, it's good to live with it for a while before we act on what we decided. This is particularly important if we have a tendency to be impulsive. We ask the Holy Spirit to give us the power and courage to act on what we believe to be God's will for our life.

6. Act on the decision.

This step can be the most difficult because it may involve giving up something to which we're still quite attached. We ask the Holy Spirit to give us courage to act on what we believe to be God's will for our life.

7. Seek confirmation of the decision.

If the choice we make bears good fruit, we can be sure we acted in accord with God's will. That's not to say that there won't be struggles or times we wonder if we made the right choice.

Knowing we made a sincere effort to seek God's will is enough. Discernment is an art learned through trial and error. God doesn't demand that we always discern perfectly; he asks only that we seek his will and act on what we discern.

> "Choose life, then, that you and your descendants may live, by loving the Lord, your God, obeying his voice, and holding fast to him. For that will mean life for you."
>
> *Deuteronomy 30:19–20*

MYSTAGOGY — JOURNEY OF FAITH

4. After prayer, you determine that you need to talk with your employer about your feelings.

5. You decide to wait a week before scheduling time to discuss these issues. What's running through your mind now?

6. You sit down with your employer and actually have the conversation.

7. After your conversation, do you feel like you've done the right thing? Were you able to be loving and firm in your stance? Does this keep you on a path that leads to a stronger relationship with God?

Discernment

JOURNEY OF FAITH | MYSTAGOGY

Helps for Discernment

1. **Living a God-centered life:** If the basic orientation is material gain, friendship, attainment of power, or pleasure, all of our choices will be made out of this orientation. Jesus' basic orientation was different.

2. **Personal knowledge of God and God's ways:** The primary way to come to a knowledge of God is through prayer and meditation on the life of Jesus.

3. **Reflective living:** Regular periods of reflective silence in the presence of God help us grow in self-knowledge and see those areas in which we're controlled by our needs, compulsions, and attachments.

4. **Genuine openness to God:** We may be locked into a narrow understanding of God and his ways. We want to truly recognize God in the person of Jesus and not settle for a version of God that's a product of our imagination.

5. **Self-knowledge:** We need to be in touch with our thoughts, feelings, and actions. We need to be aware of excessive needs and attachments that diminish our inner freedom to say "yes" to God.

- *How might regularly including God in my decision-making change my life?*

Journey of Faith for Adults: Mystagogy, M4 (826283)

Imprimi Potest: Stephen T. Rehrauer, CSsR, Provincial, Denver Province, the Redemptorists.

Imprimatur: "In accordance with CIC 827, permission to publish has been granted on June 7, 2016, by the Rev. Msgr. Mark S. Rivituso, Vicar General, Archdiocese of St. Louis. Permission to publish is an indication that nothing contrary to Church teaching is contained in this work. It does not imply any endorsement of the opinions expressed in the publication, nor is any liability assumed by this permission."

Journey of Faith for Adults © 2000, 2016 Liguori Publications, Liguori, MO 63057. All rights reserved. No part of this publication may be reproduced, distributed, stored, transmitted, or posted in any form by any means without prior written permission. To order, visit Liguori.org or call 800-325-9521. Liguori Publications, a nonprofit corporation, is an apostolate of the Redemptorists. To learn more about the Redemptorists, visit Redemptorists.com. Contributing writer: Fr. Eamon Tobin. Editors of 2016 Journey of Faith: Julia DiSalvo, Joan McKamey, and Denise Bossert. Design: Lorena Mitre Jimenez. Images: Shutterstock. Scripture texts in this work are taken from the *New American Bible*, revised edition © 2010, 1991, 1986, 1970 Confraternity of Christian Doctrine, Washington, D.C., and are used by permission of the copyright owner. All Rights Reserved. No part of the *New American Bible* may be reproduced in any form without permission in writing from the copyright owner. Excerpts from English translation of the *Catechism of the Catholic Church* for the United States of America © 1994 United States Catholic Conference, Inc.—*Libreria Editrice Vaticana*; English translation of the *Catechism of the Catholic Church: Modifications from the Editio Typica* © 1997 United States Catholic Conference, Inc.—*Libreria Editrice Vaticana*. Compliant with *The Roman Missal, Third Edition*.

Printed in the United States of America. 20 19 18 17 16 / 5 4 3 2 1. Third Edition.

Liguori PUBLICATIONS — *A Redemptorist Ministry*

Journaling

Give participants time to respond to the journal prompt. Encourage them to think of a specific area of their lives where they need help from the Holy Spirit to make a decision. Remind them that if more help is needed, they can always seek a spiritual director for guidance.

Closing Prayer

Gather around the prayer table and focus everyone's attention on the powerful symbols of the Holy Spirit present on the table. Whether or not music is available, ask the participants to bring to mind the important decisions they now face. Offer these decisions to God, and pray for the guidance of the Holy Spirit. Close with the song or pray the Glory Be together.

Take-Home

Ask participants to remember these seven steps when they are faced with an important decision, and encourage participants to journal about this decision in their prayer journal.

Discernment

M5: Our Call to Holiness

Catechism: 2012–16, 1691–98, 2028, 2427

Objectives

Participants will…

- Describe the call of all Christians to holiness.
- Define holiness as a lifelong pursuit.
- Discover that we can overcome obstacles to holiness with the help of the Holy Spirit.

Leader Meditation

1 Peter 1:15–16;
Hebrews 12:14–29

Following Jesus Christ entails becoming like Jesus Christ. We have not been called to an unapproachable kingdom, but we have been called and have encountered the unshakable kingdom, the city of the living God, a festal gathering where angels descend. We have encountered the Holy Mass, where Jesus Christ comes to each of us. He is holy. Let us pursue holiness and become like the one we receive. Where are you on this journey to holiness in Christ?

Related *Catholic Updates*

- "Saintly Sinners: Flawed but Faithful, Models of Holiness" (C1410A)
- "Saints: Holy and Human" (C9810A)
- "The Universal Call to Holiness: Empowering the Laity" (C1209A)

Leader Preparation

- Read the lesson, this lesson plan, the Scripture passage, and the *Catechism* sections.
- Find a recording of an Easter song to use for the closing prayer. Recommended song for this session is "Behold" by David Kauffman, from *Behold*, Good For the Soul Music.

Welcome

Greet neophytes as they arrive. Check for supplies and immediate needs. Solicit questions or comments about the previous sessions and/or share new information and findings. Begin promptly.

Opening Scripture

1 Peter 1:15–16;
Hebrews 12:14–29

Light the candle and read the passage aloud. Talk about the great invitation to receive Jesus Christ in the Holy Mass. If we think about the life of Christ, what do we learn about holiness and what holiness really is? What changes can we make to become more like Christ, more like this one we receive?

> "'All Christians in any state or walk of life are called to the fullness of Christian life and to the perfection of charity.' All are called to holiness: 'Be perfect, as your heavenly Father is perfect.'"
>
> CCC 2013

Journey of Faith for Adults, Enlightenment and Mystagogy Leader Guide

Journey of Faith

M5 · MYSTAGOGY · ADULTS

In Short:
- All Christians are called to holiness.
- Growth in holiness is a lifelong pursuit.
- We can overcome obstacles to holiness with the Holy Spirit's help.

"You shall love the Lord, your God, with all your heart, with all your soul, and with all your mind."

Matthew 22:37

- How would you define holiness?
- Who in your life comes to mind when you think of the word holy? Why?

Our Call to Holiness

We may squirm uncomfortably at the word *holy*, thinking it applies to our grandma, our parish priest, the pope, or Mother Teresa of Calcutta—but not to *us*. Here's a helpful equation to remember: holy ≠ perfect.

When Jesus calls disciples, he invites everyone to "the fullness of the Christian life and to the perfection of charity" (Dogmatic Constitution on the Church [*Lumen Gentium*], 40). Becoming holy means that we're in process, growing in intimacy with Christ.

All who are attracted to Jesus Christ have the grandest challenge and opportunity possible: *to become like Christ.*

Jesus said, "Blessed are they who hunger and thirst for righteousness, for they will be satisfied" (Matthew 5:6). Yet he offers no instant course in righteousness (holiness). Jesus assures us that holiness can be ours, that blessedness is promised. We have only to desire it. But we must desire it with *all* our hearts, souls, and minds:

All Are Called to Holiness

The Hebrew and Greek roots of the word *holiness* indicate *separateness* and a life that's *set apart* for God. The spiritual progress of one pursuing holiness is marked by an ever-more intimate union with Christ.

A theme running throughout the Second Vatican Council was Christ's call of *all* to a holiness that could take many forms. Whether one is a Carmelite sister or the mother of five, the Spirit provides the grace to accomplish this ultimate, wholehearted fulfillment.

Jesus is made visible in every human being, enlightening all who come into the world. Anyone who pursues good, truth, and beauty is seeking God, who is the source of these things. In each person's unique path to holiness, individual gifts and strengths play a large part.

Yet our holiness isn't solely because of anything we've done or any reward we've earned. The source of our holiness is Christ who sanctified us.

CCC 2012–16, 1691–98, 2028, 2427

Our Call to Holiness

- As a group, answer the first reflection question by coming up with a joint definition of holiness.

- Give participants time to answer the second reflection question on their own, then ask for volunteers to share. As a group, create a list of character traits that come to mind when you think of someone who is holy.

- As the group discusses holiness, emphasize the example of the saints, they loved God above all things, and wanted to be holy as he is holy, but perfection wasn't necessary for a saint to start the path to sainthood.

- Discuss the difference between striving for holiness and demanding perfection.

All Are Called to Holiness

- Emphasize that holiness is possible even for the most ordinary people. In fact, usually the simpler our lives, the more room we have for God.

- Discuss with participants how difficult (or easy) it is to consider themselves as living holy lives. Then discuss what makes it easy to see ourselves as holy and what makes it difficult.

Our Call to Holiness

Me? A Saint?

- Ask participants if they've ever felt called to become a saint. Then create a list of traits, actions, or events they think are required for becoming a saint.

- Give participants time to reflect on this discussion as they respond to the reflection questions.

Renewing Our Hearts and Minds

- As a group, create a list of things that get in the way of our desire for holiness. Then discuss ways or resources we can use to overcome those obstacles. Emphasize that reaching out to a priest, Catholic mentor, or trusted friend can help. We're more likely to stick to any goal, whether it's as important as our quest for sainthood or as simple as sticking to an exercise routine, if we have a partner to hold us accountable.

> "Blessed be the God and Father of our Lord Jesus Christ, who has blessed us in Christ with every spiritual blessing in the heavens, as he chose us in him…to be holy and without blemish before him."
>
> *Ephesians 1:3–4*

- What seeds of holiness do you see in yourself? What can you do to nurture those seeds for growth?

Me? A Saint?

In the New Testament, the word *saint* is often a synonym for *Christian*. Christians are called to belong to Jesus Christ, to be part of his holy people, *to be saints* (see Romans 1:6–7). In the epistles, Christians are often referred to as "the saints" in a given area.

The saints recognized (canonized) by the Church grew in holiness through the grace and mercy of God. Their perfecting, or sanctifying, took time and effort.

Loving God above all things and living a life centered on Jesus and the kingdom he preached is possible for each one of us. A saint says, "If I, with all my problems, can do it, with God's help, so can you."

The saints grew as we must grow. Somewhere within them they wanted holiness, and they wanted it very much. Their desire occupied their minds and changed their feelings and thoughts. Their desire was an active force in their daily activities. So they gained holiness and found the blessings of joy and peace that come with it.

Perhaps we need to stop thinking of the saints only as dead people who were perfect. God calls us to become saints, too. It may help us to think of saints as "sinners who keep on trying."

The challenge of the saints is to grow to our fullest Christian humanness. None of us is called to be more than human; but we certainly aren't called to be less. That's what sainthood is about—becoming fully human and our best possible selves, the persons God created us to be.

> "Strive…for that holiness without which no one will see the Lord."
>
> *Hebrews 12:14*

> "This is the will of God, your holiness."
>
> *1 Thessalonians 4:3*

- Why do many of us downplay our inner goodness?
- How might you shine your light more brightly if you realized you might be the only Bible some people will ever read?

Renewing Our Hearts and Minds

Jesus repeatedly tells us that it's our inner thoughts that matter, not just our external actions. The external is always powered from within:

> "Woe to you, scribes and Pharisees, you hypocrites. You cleanse the outside of cup and dish, but inside they are full of plunder and self-indulgence. Blind Pharisee, cleanse first the inside of the cup, so that the outside also may be clean."
>
> *Matthew 23:25–26*

If we truly want holiness, we'll fill our thoughts with it. We'll ponder its beauty. We'll long for its results. We'll encourage every thought that leads toward holiness. When holiness is our desire, it will become embodied in our everyday living.

Journey of Faith for Adults, Enlightenment and Mystagogy Leader Guide

If our minds and lives are cluttered with things that either don't lead us toward holiness or actually lead us away from it, holiness will have little room to grow.

Using the body as a powerful figure of speech (not to be taken literally), Jesus tells us to rid ourselves of everything that stands in the way of our pursuit of holiness:

> "If your right eye causes you to sin, tear it out and throw it away.…And if your right hand causes you to sin, cut it off and throw it away."
>
> Matthew 5:29–30

- Name something that gets in the way of your desire for holiness.

Goodness doesn't force itself upon us. Sometimes, we must purge things that become distractions in this journey to personal sanctification. When we take a trip, we want to get to a particular place. But if we take every side road we see along the way, we may never arrive. The same is true of our path to holiness. If we meander through all the distracting paths of life, we may miss the path that will lead us to the joy God desires for us.

> "All holiness consists in the love of God; but the love of God consists in conformity to the will of God; therefore, all holiness consists in conformity to the will of God."
>
> St. Alphonsus Liguori

- What do you have on your schedule this week? How can you turn those events into opportunities to grow in holiness?

The Narrow Gate

Jesus didn't tell us that becoming holy would be easy. He emphasized that it's difficult—so much so that many don't choose to reach for it:

> "Enter through the narrow gate; for the gate is wide and the road broad that leads to destruction, and those who enter through it are many. How narrow the gate and constricted the road that leads to life. And those who find it are few."
>
> Matthew 7:13–14

Somewhere within each of us, there's a tiny opening. It's hidden, but there's a way to find it. That way will be rough, but we can traverse it. Through that opening is wholeness of life, fullness of loving, fullness of peace, fullness of joy. We can have it. It's our birthright as children of God.

We can find the way and get past the obstacles of the clutter of our inner selves. We can follow the path from the opening into life. That path isn't wide and obvious, but it's there. It begins right where we are at this moment. It's peeking out from beneath and around the boulders of our distractions, mistakes, and sin.

No circumstance can keep us from holiness if we choose to enter by way of the narrow gate! For many adventures, we might need money, equipment, freedom from family responsibilities, physical stamina, or something else we don't have. But for holiness, we need only desire it and accept the help of the Holy Spirit. Jesus promised:

> "Whatever you ask the Father in my name he will give you.…Ask and you will receive, so that your joy may be complete."
>
> John 16:23–24

- In what way can the path to holiness be an adventure?

MYSTAGOGY — JOURNEY OF FAITH

Awaken Your Desire for Holiness

- As you read through the list of ways to stir the desire for holiness, invite participants to add their own holiness motivators or helps.

Our Call to Holiness

MYSTAGOGY — JOURNEY OF FAITH

Awaken Your Desire for Holiness

- **Pray.** There's never any substitute for prayer. Ask God to create in you a desire for holiness, for God and his kingdom, a desire strong enough to start you on your own path toward holiness. This is one request God will surely answer in the affirmative!

- **Take Action.** Take some definitive action toward desiring holiness. It could be a public announcement to your friends, breaking a bad habit, giving away something that's too important to you, making a change in your lifestyle or the way you do your job. Whatever it is, do it openly to provide momentum to your desire, to feed and strengthen it.

- **Ponder.** Ponder the advantages of holiness: blessedness; blissfulness; joy; peace; release from fear and worry; freedom to love and be loved without hindrance.

Make two lists.

1. List the difficulties you're facing now: fear; anxiety; conflict with your spouse, a grown child, or a coworker; confusion of priorities; worry about job or finances.

2. List the benefits holiness offers in the face of your difficulties: peace, security with God, at-oneness with self and others, clarity of purpose and direction, freedom to love, confidence and trust in God's care.

Choose holiness!

- How can I feed my hunger for wholeness and holiness?
- How will I overcome the obstacles that keep me from embracing a life of holiness?

Journey of Faith for Adults: Mystagogy, M5 (826283)
Imprimi Potest: Stephen T. Rehrauer, CSsR, Provincial, Denver Province, the Redemptorists.
Imprimatur: "In accordance with CIC 827, permission to publish has been granted on June 7, 2016, by the Rev. Msgr. Mark S. Rivituso, Vicar General, Archdiocese of St. Louis. Permission to publish is an indication that nothing contrary to Church teaching is contained in this work. It does not imply any endorsement of the opinions expressed in the publication, nor is any liability assumed by this permission."

Journey of Faith for Adults © 2000, 2016 Liguori Publications, Liguori, MO 63057. All rights reserved. No part of this publication may be reproduced, distributed, stored, transmitted, or posted in any form by any means without prior written permission. To order, visit Liguori.org or call 800-325-9521. Liguori Publications, a nonprofit corporation, is an apostolate of the Redemptorists. To learn more about the Redemptorists, visit Redemptorists.com Contributing writers: Kathy Coffey; Fr. Michael Guinan, OFM. Editors of 2016 Journey of Faith: Julia DiSalvo, Joan McKamey, and Denise Bossert. Design: Lorena Mitre Jimenez. Images: Shutterstock. Scripture texts in this work are taken from the *New American Bible*, revised edition © 2010, 1991, 1986, 1970 Confraternity of Christian Doctrine, Washington, D.C., and are used by permission of the copyright owner. All Rights Reserved. No part of the *New American Bible* may be reproduced in any form without permission in writing from the copyright owner. Excerpts from English translation of the *Catechism of the Catholic Church* for the United States of America © 1994 United States Catholic Conference, Inc.—Libreria Editrice Vaticana; English translation of the *Catechism of the Catholic Church: Modifications from the Editio Typica* © 1997 United States Catholic Conference, Inc.—Libreria Editrice Vaticana. Compliant with *The Roman Missal, Third Edition.*

Liguori PUBLICATIONS — *A Redemptorist Ministry*

Printed in the United States of America. 20 19 18 17 16 / 5 4 3 2 1. Third Edition.

Journey of Faith for Adults, Enlightenment and Mystagogy Leader Guide

Journaling

Give participants time to complete the journal prompt this session. Then invite them to create an original prayer asking God for his help and grace to overcome obstacles and become more like Christ.

Closing Prayer

Gather the group in a circle around the prayer table and remind them that we are all called to holiness. Have them consider the saints and especially the Blessed Mother. Ask for their intercession before the throne of God that we might join their ranks as saints among the saints. Then listen to a recording of "Behold" by David Kauffman, from *Behold*, Good For the Soul Music. If music is unavailable, offer silent thanksgiving for these special people and pray together the Lord's Prayer and the Glory Be.

Looking Ahead

As participants begin to think about holiness, ask them to also think about those good habits or virtues that make the path to holiness smoother. Let participants know you'll be talking about this more in your next session.

Our Call to Holiness

M6: Living the Virtues

Catechism: 1804–1829

Objectives

Participants will…

- Discover that God's ways are manifested in the lives of those who practice the virtues.
- Differentiate between the human and theological virtues.
- Identify the greatest of the virtues as love (charity).

Leader Meditation

Philippians 4:8–9

It is not easy to live out the virtues when we live in a world in which people are prone to gossip, to be materialistic, and to indulge a desire for immediate self-gratification. We are called to a higher purpose. We were meant for something more. How deeply do you live this life in Christ? On a day-to-day basis, does your life conform to the world or does it seek to live out the virtues?

Related *Catholic Updates*

- "The Beatitudes: Finding Where Your Treasure Is" (C9112A)
- "Responding to Tragedy With Hope and Love" (C1504A)
- "God Is Love" (C0604A)

Leader Preparation

- Read the lesson, this lesson plan, the Scripture passage, and the *Catechism* sections.
- Find a recording of a song to use for the closing prayer. Recommend song for this session is "Prayer of St. Francis" by Vince Ambrosetti, from Sacred Song, International Liturgy Publications.
- Be familiar with the vocabulary terms for this lesson: virtues, human virtues, theological virtues, corporal works of mercy, spiritual works of mercy. Definitions are provided in this guide's glossary.

Welcome

Greet neophytes as they arrive. Check for supplies and immediate needs. Solicit questions or comments about the previous sessions and/or share new information and findings. Begin promptly.

Opening Scripture

Philippians 4:8–9

Light the candle and read the passage aloud. Talk about our ultimate purpose: to be everything God meant for us to be when he created us. Compare and contrast the life we are called to live (based on this passage from sacred Scripture) and the standard the world sets before us.

> "[Virtue] allows the person not only to perform good acts, but to give the best of himself….The goal of a virtuous life is to become like God."
>
> CCC 1804

Journey of Faith for Adults, Enlightenment and Mystagogy Leader Guide

M6 MYSTAGOGY

In Short:
- God's ways are manifested in the lives of those who practice the virtues.
- There are both human virtues and theological virtues.
- The greatest of the virtues is love (charity), which orders all the other virtues.

A virtue is a good habit, an ongoing "and firm disposition to do the good" (CCC 1803).

"Since we are surrounded by so great a cloud of witnesses, let us rid ourselves of every burden and sin that clings to us and persevere in running the race that lies before us while keeping our eyes fixed on Jesus, the leader and perfecter of faith."

Hebrews 12:1–2

Living the Virtues

Habits are patterns of behavior or thought. We're all too familiar with bad habits; we may even call them *vices*. **Virtues** are nurtured attitudes and efforts to do good and give the best of ourselves. They aren't merit badges to be earned and worn to prove our goodness. Rather, they're dispositions that shape us into the people God created us to be.

> "Whatever is true, whatever is honorable, whatever is just, whatever is pure, whatever is lovely, whatever is gracious, if there is any excellence and if there is anything worthy of praise, think about these things."
>
> *Philippians 4:8*

Virtuous people freely choose to cooperate with the grace of God. Catholic Tradition distinguishes between human, also known as moral or cardinal, virtues and theological virtues. **Human virtues** are acquired through our human efforts. They "govern our actions, order our passions, and guide our conduct" (CCC 1804). **Theological virtues** are gifts from God, who is "their origin, motive, and object" (CCC 1812). Both the human and theological virtues are characteristics of followers of Christ.

The Human (Moral or Cardinal) Virtues

Prudence
The prudent person examines a situation closely, considers all options, and chooses the option that leads toward the greatest good.

Sometimes people mistake prudence for excessive caution or restraint. However, the prudent person is prepared to make the right decision when the time arrives. Furthermore, prudence is judged not simply on whether the action produces some good (the end) but also whether that choice, in its whole context (including the means), is the best possible action.

Prudence guides and steers the other virtues by setting boundaries and standards that lead to right judgment.

Justice
Justice is right action or right relationship. It directs us to consistently and firmly give what's due to God and neighbor. There will always be some inequality, inconsistency, or disharmony in our human relationships. Perfect justice will come from God at the Final Judgment.

CCC 1804–29

ADULTS

Living the Virtues
- Review the definition of virtue as presented in the lesson.
- Discuss the difference in the way we obtain human virtues versus theological virtues.
- We acquire the human virtues through our human effort in cooperation with grace as we try to live more like Christ. We acquire the theological virtues wholly as gifts from God.

The Human (Moral or Cardinal) Virtues
- Pause after each virtue to reflect on the questions in the lesson. Encourage discussion. Some of the reflection questions are of a personal nature. Consider giving the participants time to respond to these questions in their prayer journal.
- After you discuss each virtue, ask participants to come up with a scenario in which that virtue would be needed and why.

Living the Virtues

The Theological Virtues

- Pause after each virtue to reflect on the questions in the lesson. Encourage discussion. Some of the reflection questions are of a personal nature. Consider giving the participants time to respond to these questions in their prayer journal.

- After you discuss each virtue, ask participants to come up with a scenario in which that virtue would be needed and why.

JOURNEY OF FAITH — MYSTAGOGY

Some people think being just means giving the same to everyone, dividing things equally. Others think justice means giving people what they've earned. Payment based on merit is appropriate, yet Jesus told a parable of a vineyard owner who went out at five different times of day to hire workers. At the end of the day, he paid all the workers a full day's wage. The workers who had worked all day were outraged to receive the same daily wage as those who had worked less. They couldn't comprehend a master who responded with generosity, a generosity that goes beyond mere recompense (see Matthew 20:1–16).

- When has one of your children (or a sibling) needed something different than the other children?
- When have you felt that your employer was unfair to you when dealing with a fellow employee? Is it possible the appearance of favoritism was a matter of meeting the needs of an employee in a unique way?

Fortitude

Fortitude enables us to endure difficulties in our pursuit of the good with courage and purpose. While prudence and justice guide the reasoning process, fortitude and temperance help us follow through.

Fear or self-doubt may tempt us to abandon action, our family might oppose our commitment to social justice, or peer pressure can sway us from choosing what's right. In all instances, however, the person of fortitude will persist in pursuing the good.

- When have you been tempted to choose poorly because of fear or peer pressure?

Temperance

A key word for temperance is *balance*. Temperance deflects the excessive attraction of human pleasures and provides moderation in exercising one's passion. It provides balance in the use of goods and gifts and "ensures the will's mastery over instincts and keeps desires within the limits of what is honorable" (*CCC* 1809).

Temperance asks us to measure carefully our use of created goods, not to avoid them entirely. The Gospel calls us to the reasonable use of material goods, money in particular. A lack of balance often leads to consumerism, materialism, and amassing possessions while missing life's deeper purpose.

Understanding temperance as moderation or balance is especially important when we're dealing with emotions, which are critical in the moral life. They spark the initial movement toward the good. Yet, they must be measured, channeled, and ordered toward the good.

- Name a temptation or challenge you face regularly. What is a small step you can take to reduce its power over you?

The Theological Virtues

The theological virtues originate in God, are effective under his direction, and have him as their destiny. Authentic human good and union with God go together. We can experience a degree of contentment in this life, but genuine happiness comes through union with God.

The journey toward union with God can't be made on human effort alone. The virtues help us find our way home to the Father, but we'll continue to bump up against the limits of human frailty and sin. Faith, hope, and charity move us out of ourselves and help us grow in holiness and practice the moral virtues.

"To ask about the good...ultimately means to turn towards God, the fullness of goodness."

Pope St. John Paul II, *The Splendor of Truth*, 9

Journey of Faith for Adults, Enlightenment and Mystagogy Leader Guide

Faith

Faith enables us to believe in God and hold as true all that he has revealed. It allows us to acknowledge God's existence *and* fall in love with God who first loved us.

As a gift, faith must be received and nurtured. No one becomes faith-filled upon acknowledging God's existence or reciting a creed. Since faith is about friendship with God, it's sustained and strengthened in proportion to our efforts to build personal relationship with God. Faith grows as we make time for Christ and as we encounter the community of believers who make up the Church.

There are two main consequences of faith:

- *A good moral life.* Our image of God is false if we think we can believe in God and not have concern for others. There's a necessary link between believing in God and right moral action.

- *A spirit of evangelization.* It's difficult to keep good news to ourselves. We want to share good news so that others may share our joy. The same dynamic is at work within the faithful. They share the good news of salvation in Christ with others.

Faith prompts not only a spirit of humility and gratitude but also of determination to become who God has created us to be.

- What impact has your growing faith had on your life so far?

Hope

Hope is born of confidence in God's presence and activity in the world. Hope instills a joyful longing for the coming of God's kingdom. Hope that God will bring to completion the good work begun in us helps us to courageously pursue the good.

"[Hope] keeps man from discouragement; it sustains him during times of abandonment; it opens up his heart in expectation of eternal beatitude. Buoyed up by hope, he is preserved from selfishness and led to the happiness that flows from charity."

CCC 1818

Charity (Love)

Charity is "the source and the goal of [our] Christian practice" (CCC 1827). Created from Love itself, we are made for love. It orders all the other virtues because it's the goal toward which they all strive. Charity involves receiving God's love into our hearts and loving God and neighbor in response.

Saint Thomas Aquinas wrote that to love someone is to make their loves and concerns our own. Jesus says, "As I have loved you, so you also should love one another" (John 13:34). With so many contemporary notions of love, the witness and love of Jesus provides the reference point for the way we are to love. The Lord asks us to love "even our *enemies*, to make ourselves the neighbor of those farthest away, and to love children and the poor as Christ himself" (CCC 1825).

"So faith, hope, love remain, these three; but the greatest of these is love."

1 Corinthians 13:13

Practicing the Virtues

- Emphasize that the spiritual and corporal works of mercy are tangible expressions of the virtuous life.

- As a group, reflect on each of the spiritual and corporal works of mercy and consider which virtues equip and prepare us to fulfill each work. If you have time, create a chart or graph to capture participants' responses.

- Then, ask participants to identify which works are a good fit with their personality and have them capture these thoughts in their prayer journal.

Living the Virtues

MYSTAGOGY | JOURNEY OF FAITH

Practicing the Virtues

Living the virtues means practicing the **Corporal and Spiritual Works of Mercy**.

Corporal Works of Mercy

- Feed the hungry.
- Give drink to the thirsty.
- Clothe the naked.
- Shelter the homeless.
- Visit the sick.
- Visit the imprisoned.
- Bury the dead.

Spiritual Works of Mercy

- Instruct the ignorant.
- Counsel the doubtful.
- Admonish the sinner.
- Bear wrongs patiently.
- Forgive offenses willingly.
- Comfort the afflicted.
- Pray for the living and the dead.

- How do/can I model or reflect the virtues in my life?
- Which of the works of mercy is calling me to action?

Journey of Faith for Adults: Mystagogy, M6 (826283)
Imprimi Potest: Stephen T. Rehrauer, CSsR, Provincial, Denver Province, the Redemptorists.
Imprimatur: "In accordance with CIC 827, permission to publish has been granted on June 7, 2016, by the Rev. Msgr. Mark S. Rivituso, Vicar General, Archdiocese of St. Louis. Permission to publish is an indication that nothing contrary to Church teaching is contained in this work. It does not imply any endorsement of the opinions expressed in the publication, nor is any liability assumed by this permission."
Journey of Faith for Adults © 2000, 2016 Liguori Publications, Liguori, MO 63057. All rights reserved. No part of this publication may be reproduced, distributed, stored, transmitted, or posted in any form by any means without prior written permission. To order, visit Liguori.org or call 800-325-9521. Liguori Publications, a nonprofit corporation, is an apostolate of the Redemptorists. To learn more about the Redemptorists, visit Redemptorists.com. Editors of 2016 Journey of Faith: Julia DiSalvo, Joan McKamey, and Denise Bossert. Design: Lorena Jimenez. Images: Shutterstock. Excerpted and adapted from *The Essential Moral Handbook* by Kevin O'Neil, CSsR, and Peter Black, CSsR. Scripture texts in this work are taken from the *New American Bible*, revised edition © 2010, 1991, 1986, 1970 Confraternity of Christian Doctrine, Washington, D.C., and are used by permission of the copyright owner. All Rights Reserved. No part of the *New American Bible* may be reproduced in any form without permission in writing from the copyright owner. Excerpts from English translation of the *Catechism of the Catholic Church* for the United States of America © 1994 United States Catholic Conference, Inc.—Libreria Editrice Vaticana; English translation of the *Catechism of the Catholic Church: Modifications from the Editio Typica* © 1997 United States Catholic Conference, Inc.—Libreria Editrice Vaticana. Compliant with *The Roman Missal, Third Edition*.

LIGUORI PUBLICATIONS
A Redemptorist Ministry

Printed in the United States of America. 20 19 18 17 16 / 5 4 3 2 1. Third Edition.

Journaling

Encourage participants to use your discussion about the spiritual and corporal works of mercy to answer the journal prompt this session. If you don't have time left in the session to journal, ask participants to complete do so at home.

Closing Prayer

Gather the group in a circle around the prayer table. Pray the Prayer of St. Francis.

Looking Ahead

Ask participants to spend time between now and the next session looking for examples of virtue in action at home and in their family members.

M7: Family Life

Catechism: 2201–13

Objectives

Participants will...

- Identify the family as the domestic church.
- Describe parents as the first and most important teachers of the faith.
- Examine how families can grow in faith through family rituals and traditions.

Leader Meditation

Colossians 3:12–21

Verses 12 through 17 of this passage help us to better understand the directives found in verses 18 through 21. Think about the relationships you have with the members of your own family, especially those who may present special challenges. Pray for those virtues needed to make your home a place of warmth, peace, and love.

Related *Catholic Updates*

- "Faith-Sharing in the Family" (C1408A)
- "Five 'Marks' of Today's Catholic Family" (C1608A)
- "Helping Our Children Grow in Faith" (C8209A)
- "Seeing Family Life as Holy, Warts and All" (C9210A)

Leader Preparation

- Read the lesson, this lesson plan, the Scripture passage, and the *Catechism* sections.
- Recording of an Easter hymn or song used frequently in Masses at your parish.
- Be familiar with the vocabulary term for this lesson: catechesis. The definition is provided in this guide's glossary.

Welcome

Greet participants as they arrive. Check for supplies and immediate needs. Solicit questions or comments about the previous sessions and/or share new information and findings. Begin promptly.

Opening Scripture

Colossians 3:12–21

Light the candle and read the passage aloud. (You may prefer to use two readers—one for verses 12–17 and another for verses 18–21.) Encourage a discussion about ways that each family member can follow these directives in the name of love.

> "'The Christian family constitutes a specific revelation and realization of ecclesial communion, and for this reason it can and should be called a domestic church.'" It is a community of faith, hope, and charity; it assumes singular importance in the Church, as is evident in the New Testament."
>
> CCC 2204

Journey of Faith for Adults, Enlightenment and Mystagogy Leader Guide

Journey of Faith

M7 MYSTAGOGY

In Short:
- The family is the "domestic Church."
- Parents are their children's first and most important teachers of the faith.
- Families can grow in faith through family rituals and traditions.

Family Life

We naturally want what's best for the children in our family. Society's messages can lead us to think that fame, power, physical beauty, financial security, perfect health, success, wealth, and influence are what's "best" and most desirable. While each of these things has its perks, we likely see deeper and more lasting value in internal characteristics such as patience, kindness, goodness, generosity, self-respect, compassion, tolerance, integrity, and honesty.

It's our job as adult family members, through our love, care, influence, and example, to lay the foundation that will encourage a child to develop these deeper and more lasting characteristics.

That's why the Catholic Church puts so much emphasis on the importance of family life. A happy and stable family provides the kind of atmosphere in which a child learns to relate to others: to care, share, love, and forgive.

- What do you hope the children in your family will learn from you? Why?

First Teachers of the Faith

It's within the family that children learn they're loved and accepted. This forms the basis of their image of themselves, their relationships with other people, and their relationship with God.

Parents are their children's first and most important teachers. In this role, they are never off duty. Everything they do and say rubs off on their children and has an influence for good or bad. The way they speak, treat others, cope with disagreements, and show tolerance and forgiveness are all very important.

> "The family is...the domestic church. In it parents should, by their word and example, be the first preachers of the faith to their children."
>
> Dogmatic Constitution on the Church (Lumen Gentium), 11

> "Education in the faith by the parents should begin in the child's earliest years. This already happens when family members help one another to grow in faith by the witness of a Christian life....Parents have the mission of teaching their children to pray and to discover their vocation as children of God."
>
> CCC 2226

- In what ways did your parents or other significant adults serve as role models for you? What are some of the main lessons you learned from their example?

ADULTS

CCC 2201-13

Family Life
- Read the introduction to this lesson together. Discuss what participants hope their children or other members of their family will learn from them.

First Teachers of the Faith
- As you begin this lesson, remember to be sensitive to participants coming from especially difficult or irregular family circumstances.
- Ask participants to answer the first reflection question on their own. Then ask each participant to name at least one trait they admired in their influencers growing up. Capture responses somewhere.
- As a group, discuss ways the home can be transformed into the domestic Church for their families. For single participants, encourage them to think how their home can be a domestic Church for friends and relatives, as well as a place of ongoing faith formation for them individually.

Building a Christian Framework

- The lesson handout includes some ways parents can build a Christian framework with their children. As a group, brainstorm more ideas that would be easy to implement at home.

MYSTAGOGY — JOURNEY OF FAITH

Building a Christian Framework

In today's world, it's challenging to bring up a family within a Christian framework. The values of a consumer society are often opposed to the values of Jesus Christ. Difficult sacrifices may be required. At times, we may feel under pressure because we can't keep up the standard of living we'd like or give our children all the things they want. But we have a much greater gift to give: the love, security, and life/faith lessons of a happy home.

Here are some ways we can pass on our faith to our families:

Scripture Storytelling

Just about everyone loves a good story. Notice how people's posture changes at Mass when the priest or deacon starts the homily with a story. Some will sit back, relax, and expect to enjoy and be engaged. Others may lean forward as a sign of their interest. Stories are powerful tools for making a point in a way that's memorable and enjoyable.

Children love stories, too—both hearing and telling them. Young listeners are entertained, enlightened, and inspired; imaginations are awakened, and a bond forms between listener and storyteller. No wonder Jesus so often taught with parables!

Breaking Scripture into simple stories can give children a personal image of Jesus. By selecting stories from the Mass, we can also encourage them to listen more attentively at Mass. We can study the readings to find the "story element" and re-present it in a child-sized package. Making it "their story" is an important step in a **catechesis** that establishes them on their faith journey.

Mass Helps

Mass isn't an easy activity for most children—or their parents! Little ones can get restless, and older ones can become bored. Here a few tricks that might help:

- Practice Scripture storytelling at home.
- Stop by church for a show-and-tell visit. Kneel together for quiet prayer before you leave.
- Before Mass, talk to your children about coming up with their own special petition and encourage them to bring it to Jesus at Mass.
- Purchase a Mass book for each child. For younger ones, choose a book with pictures to help them follow along visually.
- Show children how to make the sign of the cross with holy water when you enter the church.
- Choose a pew near the sanctuary so they can see what's going on. It's hard to be holy while staring at people's backs.
- Give younger children money for the collection. Older ones should give their own. Explain how the Church uses their money. Help them identify ministries they care about.
- Take small children with you when you receive Communion.

- What is your experience of sharing your faith with a child?
- How might you offer support to parents of young children at Mass?

Journey of Faith for Adults, Enlightenment and Mystagogy Leader Guide

Moments That Matter

The hectic pace of today's society cries out for time to be quiet with God. But with homework, Church involvement, jobs, school, and sports activities, when can busy parents fit it in?

Bedtime
A widowed mother of four finds her moment at bedtime. Her children sit on her bed while they read together. Then they pray a decade of the rosary with emphasis on the story behind the mystery. After adding personal prayers, it's a kiss and off to bed.

Mealtime
For larger families with teenagers, dinner may be the only together time. To make it a special moment, slow down the mealtime blessing. Light a candle, perhaps read a short passage from the Bible, and have a child offer the blessing.

A divorced father may choose Sunday morning for his moments. The morning might begin with a big breakfast and discussion about the Gospel reading, liturgical season, or upcoming holy day. Some Sundays, they may go out for lunch and talk about how they see God at work in their lives.

Anniversary of Baptism
Families may celebrate the anniversary of a child's baptism. Bring out photos, the baptismal candle, and the white garment. Talk about who was there, how you celebrated, whether the child cried or slept through it all. Give the child a small present such as a rosary, prayer book, a saint prayer card, or medal to mark the day as special.

Forgiveness
Children learn to offer, seek, and accept forgiveness within the family. Parents must model this for their children—through openly admitting fault, offering an apology, and asking for and offering forgiveness. Reminding children of God's and their parents' great love and desire for reconciliation will help them internalize this important reality of our faith.

Make time for the sacrament of reconciliation. Go as a family and pray for each other and for forgiveness of family hurts. Celebrate afterward by going to the park or having cake and ice cream.

- *What are some of the key learning moments from your own childhood? What did you learn about yourself, others, the world, and God as a result?*

Family Prayer

Family prayer time helps children make God central to daily life. Our prayer is an ongoing dialogue with our loving God. Whether memorized or spontaneous, the dialogue of prayer must be practiced, modeled, and encouraged.

Establish a family prayer plan. Begin with a moment of silence. Help children connect with God. When we share a spontaneous prayer such as "Thank you, God, for being with Jonathan during his test today," we make a quick connection with God for our children.

Opportunities to make our children more aware of God's presence can happen naturally. Encourage them to invite God to be with them as they study. Send them off to school with a blessing. At bedtime, ease their fears by assuring them of God's constant care. (If nighttime fears are a big concern, teach them the Guardian Angel Prayer.) By bringing everyday feelings and events to God in prayer, we help children recognize God's continual presence and create occasions for the God-child relationship to grow.

- *How comfortable are you with praying with members of your family? Why?*

MYSTAGOGY | JOURNEY OF FAITH

Moments That Matter

- As a group, use the examples in the lesson handout to jump start a discussion on other important moments family members can turn into a time of faith formation and growth.

Family Life

MYSTAGOGY — JOURNEY OF FAITH

Saintly Role Models

If our children want to be athletes, musicians, or artists, we encourage them. We buy instruments or equipment and sign them up for lessons or a team. We introduce them to good role models within their area of interest.

The need for good examples or role models is also important in the area of Christian living. For this purpose, the Church encourages devotion to the saints. To enkindle a desire for Christian greatness, read to children about the lives of the saints. These models of virtuous living will encourage children to put the same virtues into practice in their daily lives.

Choose a family "saint of the week" and find creative ways to emulate and celebrate that saint. Imitate Mother Teresa's care for others by visiting the sick or making cards for shut-ins. Imitate Francis of Assisi's love of nature by building a backyard bird feeder or taking a prayer walk in the woods. An Italian saint's day might be celebrated with an Italian dinner (or a Spanish dish for John of the Cross or French pastries for Thérèse of Lisieux).

Saints offer more than just their example. Explain that we belong to a special club, the communion of saints. As members of this club, children can call on those already in heaven to pray for them and help them every day.

God's love can be found right in our homes—around the kitchen table, in the family room, at the backyard barbecue.

- When have you felt God's presence in your family? What can you do to promote this awareness?

Journey of Faith for Adults: Mystagogy, M7 (826293)
Imprimi Potest: Stephen T. Rehrauer, CSsR, Provincial, Denver Province, the Redemptorists.
Imprimatur: "In accordance with CIC 827, permission to publish has been granted on June 7, 2016, by the Rev. Msgr. Mark S. Rivituso, Vicar General, Archdiocese of St. Louis. Permission to publish is an indication that nothing contrary to Church teaching is contained in this work. It does not imply any endorsement of the opinions expressed in the publication; nor is any liability assumed by this permission."
Journey of Faith for Adults © 2000, 2016 Liguori Publications, Liguori, MO 63057. All rights reserved. No part of this publication may be reproduced, distributed, stored, transmitted, or posted in any form by any means without prior written permission. To order, visit Liguori.org or call 800-325-9521. Liguori Publications, a nonprofit corporation, is an apostolate of the Redemptorists. To learn more about the Redemptorists, visit Redemptorists.com. Contributing writers: Fr. Michael Henesy, CSsR; Francine O'Connor; William Rabior. Editors of 2016 Journey of Faith: Julia DiSalvo, Joan McKamey, and Denise Bossert. Design: Lorena Mitre Jimenez. Images: Shutterstock. Scripture texts in this work are taken from the New American Bible, revised edition © 2010, 1991, 1986, 1970 Confraternity of Christian Doctrine, Washington, D.C., and are used by permission of the copyright owner. All Rights Reserved. No part of the New American Bible may be reproduced in any form without permission in writing from the copyright owner. Excerpts from English translation of the Catechism of the Catholic Church for the United States of America © 1994 United States Catholic Conference, Inc.—Libreria Editrice Vaticana; English translation of the Catechism of the Catholic Church: Modifications from the Editio Typica © 1997 United States Catholic Conference, Inc.—Libreria Editrice Vaticana. Compliant with The Roman Missal, Third Edition.

LIGUORI PUBLICATIONS
A Redemptorist Ministry   Printed in the United States of America. 20 19 18 17 16 / 5 4 3 2 1. Third Edition.

Journey of Faith for Adults, Enlightenment and Mystagogy Leader Guide

Journaling

As participants being to work on their journal prompt for this session, encourage them to think about the call to share the faith with others, especially those closest to them. In addition to journaling about faith-sharing in the family, invite participants to extend the prompt to times they've felt God's presence with friends, in the workplace, or in their community.

Closing Prayer

Conclude with the song you've chosen for today's session. If music isn't available, pray a decade of the Rosary together, as family in the Body of Christ.

Take-Home

Try one of the tricks of the trade in the section "Mass Helps." If you do not have children, consider implementing one of these suggestions as part of your own preparation for Mass. Since prayer is key to a spiritual foundation for the family, begin adding a decade of the rosary to your family bedtime ritual. As your family grows in the faith or when your family hits those difficult times and your faith is tested, continue to practice the suggestions you have implemented.

M8: Evangelization

Catechism: 429, 849–56, 901–13, 2471–74

Objectives

Participants will...

- Realize that a relationship with Jesus Christ is fundamental to conversion.
- Develop their call to share the good news.
- Discover the ways the Church prepares and strengthens us for the ongoing mission of evangelization.

Leader Meditation

Reflect on this excerpt from Matthew Kilmurry's *You Are the Catholic Brand*:

You represent the Catholic Christian brand to everyone you meet. We often believe it's solely the responsibility of those living religious life. But in reality, the Catholic brand also belongs to lay Catholics who live, work, and play in the world outside the Church. You have been given tremendous power as a Catholic. Whether you know it or not, you are wielding that power at all times. There is no "off" button. Your influence is always "on" even if you don't feel like a good Catholic.

Ask yourself, "What Catholic brand do I show the world? How can I become more aware of the ways my actions influence others about the faith?" Pray for wisdom and guidance as you continue the work of evangelization within the Church.

Related *Catholic Updates*

- "Five Ways to Share Your Faith" (C1401A)
- "The Joy of Being Catholic" (C1405A)

Leader Preparation

- Read the lesson, this lesson plan, the Opening Reading, and the *Catechism* sections.
- Be familiar with the vocabulary terms for this lesson: evangelization, witness. Definitions can be found in this guide's glossary.
- Meet with the hospitality team to organize light refreshments to celebrate the end of the neophytes' RCIA process.
- Invite the pastor to attend this final session in order to celebrate with the group and to bless the neophytes and RCIA team.

Welcome

Greet the neophytes as they arrive. Solicit questions or comments about any of the previous sessions and/or share any final information and findings. Begin promptly.

Opening Reading

Invite a volunteer to read this excerpt from Matthew Kilmurry's *You Are the Catholic Brand*:

A Brand Evangelist is someone so in love with a brand, a product, or a place that they do unofficial marketing for it. There's nothing more powerful for promotion. Who hasn't encountered a passionate fan of a movie, car, restaurant, or band? Their enthusiasm is contagious. Through that fan you live a transformational experience. All you need is the look on their face....This is true in our spiritual lives also. Those of us who are converts often feel unequipped to pass along the faith because we don't always know the details of our faith like the exact scripture quotes for a given situation or the accurate historical accounts. We are left paralyzed. But just as the Brand Evangelist doesn't know the ingredients of the pizza sauce or the car's suspension, we have to remember that all those details about the faith aren't the only thing people are attracted to. People are looking for an unforgettable experience. They're looking for conversion.

- Ask participants, "Have you ever been such a fan of something that you tend to mention and recommend it to everyone around you?"

"It is from God's love for all men that the Church in every age receives both the obligation and the vigor of her missionary dynamism, 'for the love of Christ urges us on.'...They proclaim the Good News to those who do not know it, in order to consolidate, complete, and raise up the truth and the goodness that God has distributed." — *CCC* 851, 856

Journey of Faith for Adults, Enlightenment and Mystagogy Leader Guide

Journey of Faith

M8 · MYSTAGOGY · ADULTS

In Short:
- A relationship with Jesus is fundamental to conversion.
- We are called to share the good news.
- The Church prepares us for the mission of evangelization.

Evangelization is something God calls all the baptized to do. As Pope Francis wrote in the Joy of the Gospel (*Evangelii Gaudium*), "We know well that with Jesus life becomes richer and that with him it is easier to find meaning in everything. This is why we evangelize" (*EG* 266). Evangelization becomes part of us, part of who we are, so much so that we sometimes evangelize without even realizing we're doing it.

- *Did another person help introduce you to the Catholic faith? Describe your encounter with this person.*

Evangelization

"One day at lunch, a group of us started talking about religion. I started challenging Margaret, who was Catholic. I thought I knew what Catholics believed. Margaret very patiently explained what Catholic beliefs really are. Years later, I remembered what she said."

"I'd been going to a Catholic church for a couple of weeks but felt out of place so I just sat by myself. One day, a woman introduced herself and helped make me feel like I belonged."

"After my brother became Catholic, he sent me a lot of books by Merton, Chesterton, and others. I just put them on a shelf. One day years later, I started to read those books, and they made sense."

In each example, a Catholic was evangelizing. We've all encountered people like them, people who witness to the good news of the gospel of Jesus Christ.

What Is Evangelization?

Evangelization comes from the Greek for "to bring or to announce the good news." To evangelize means to testify and proclaim the mystery of God's salvation of humanity in Christ Jesus.

Evangelization involves much more than bringing the gospel to people who've never heard the good news. It also means bringing Christians to a deeper awareness of Jesus Christ and his love for them. Through evangelization, *hearers* of the word of God become better equipped to become *doers* of the word. Thus, evangelization forms the basis for all ministry within the Church.

Evangelization is a concept as old as Christianity itself. Christ's last words to us before ascending into heaven were about evangelizing:

CCC 429, 849–856, 901–913, 2471–74

Evangelization

- Invite the participants to share about a person who was instrumental in drawing them to the Catholic Church. Consider broadening the subject to individuals who supported them through the RCIA process or developing a brief, informal "thank-you" ritual for sponsors and godparents. Encourage them to record these relationships and experiences in their journal and to reach out to these mentors and friends regularly.

What Is Evangelization?

- Proclaim Acts 11:19–26. Explain that the early Church evangelized through *relationship*: preaching, witness (faith sharing), and personal invitation. As people listened and believed, their faith grew and they joined with other Christians in the Church. When we share our faith with others through our words and actions, we continue the mission of these first disciples.

- Ask participants to think about the influences in their lives who have led them to the Church. Create a list of traits all these influencers had in common.

- Invite participants to use this list as a jumping off point as they answer the reflection questions.

How Do We Evangelize?

- Point out that evangelization, like conversion, is a process. It requires time, patience, dedication, and love. Emphasize that, like holiness, evangelization can occur in the simplest of circumstances and can never be forced or rushed. Evangelists shouldn't be pushy or offensive.

- Have the neophytes take turns reading the five steps. Discuss each step using the lesson's questions as a starting point.

Step One: Witness Christ

- Mention to participants that some say, "To evangelize, one must be evangelized." Ask them, "What does that mean to you? Do you agree with this statement? Why or why not?"

JOURNEY OF FAITH | MYSTAGOGY

"Go, therefore, and make disciples of all nations, baptizing them in the name of the Father, and of the Son, and of the holy Spirit, teaching them to observe all that I have commanded you."

Matthew 28:19–20

For someone to become a disciple of Christ, it helps if they have a relationship with a person who has already embraced the good news and is a member of the Church. That can make a crucial difference.

- Who has been that person in your life?
- Can you begin to see how you might become that kind of person for another?

How Do We Evangelize?

Here's a five-step plan for evangelization based on the teachings of Pope Paul VI in On Evangelization in the Modern World (*Evangelii Nuntiandi*). All quotations in this lesson not otherwise cited are from this document.

Step One: *Witness Christ*

Our first step in becoming evangelizers is to live lives that **witness** our faith in Christ to those around us. Pope Paul VI pointed out that "Modern [people listen] more willingly to witnesses than to teachers, and if [they do] listen to teachers, it is because they are witnesses" (*EN* 41).

The positive witness of a loving, caring, and forgiving Catholic is the strongest method of attracting people to Jesus and the Church. Love is our most powerful argument for conversion. It will lead others to Jesus Christ.

- In what ways may you be called to share the good news of Jesus' love for those around you?

Step Two: *Share Our Faith*

The second step in evangelization is explaining the teachings of Christ in terms of what it means to be Catholic. Silent witness isn't enough, for "even the finest witness will prove ineffective...if it is not explained, justified...and made explicit by a clear and unequivocal proclamation of the Lord Jesus" (*EN* 22).

Jesus was the greatest witness that ever lived, yet his witness wouldn't have reached us if he hadn't ceaselessly explained what salvation means for daily life. His Sermon on the Mount, parables, and dialogues with people show us how to share what we believe.

Many Catholics are hesitant to evangelize. Bible studies, adult faith formation programs, and small faith-sharing and prayer groups are all great opportunities for sharing our faith. These activities increase participants' confidence and comfort in explaining and sharing Catholic teachings. The more a Catholic studies and understands the Bible, especially in a community setting, the more active that Catholic will be as an evangelizer.

- What activities might help you become a better evangelizer?

"The person who has been evangelized goes on to evangelize others....It is unthinkable that a person should accept the Word and give himself to the kingdom without becoming a person who bears witness to it and proclaims it in his turn" (*EN* 24).

Journey of Faith for Adults, Enlightenment and Mystagogy Leader Guide

Step Three: *Offer the Option for Love*

Pope John Paul II told America's youth on a visit to the United States, "I propose to you the option of love, which is the opposite of escape. If you really accept that love from Christ, it will lead you to God" (Mass on Boston Common, October 1, 1979).

This is the third step in evangelization, the core content of our sharing: "To evangelize is first of all to bear witness, in a simple and direct way, to God revealed by Jesus Christ, in the Holy Spirit" (EN 26).

The best way to do this is on a person-to-person basis. People attract people. Love begets love. Faith in action becomes love, and love takes the shape of service. The greatest service we can give is to offer Christ's invitation to salvation from death and sin through a life of love, justice, and mercy.

- With whom might you be called to share Jesus Christ? A spouse? A friend? A child? A coworker?

Evangelization = Love

Pope Paul VI reminds us that to evangelize is to love. He notes three signs of love in the process of evangelization:

1. Respect for the religious and spiritual situation of those being evangelized.
2. Concern not to wound the person, especially if that person is weak in faith.
3. Effort to transmit not doubts and uncertainties arising out of improper study and incomplete knowledge, but certainties that are anchored in the word of God (see EN 79).

Step Four: *Challenge Our Culture*

Our Catholic witness should affect the values of our society, causing us to be countercultural when necessary. Evangelization involves "affecting and… upsetting, through the power of the Gospel, mankind's criteria of judgment, determining values, points of interest, lines of thought, sources of inspiration and models of life, which are in contrast with the Word of God and the plan of salvation" (EN 19).

Jesus challenged the hypocrisy of those who planned to stone the woman accused of adultery. He spoke against the powerful who would lay burdens on the poor. He condemned religious leaders who reduced the faith to minor practices and "neglected the weightier things of the law: judgment and mercy and fidelity" (Matthew 23:23).

Jesus asks us to bring the gospel to bear on our society, to speak up on behalf of the poor and the homeless, to strengthen the place of marriage and family, to raise our children with a spirit of peace, and to hold dear the virtue of forming nonviolent societies. We cannot segregate our religious life from life in our culture, for the hidden energy of the gospel has the power to transform culture.

- To which of these areas of the culture might the Holy Spirit be calling you to assist in a work of gospel transformation?

Evangelization = Love

- Review the points made by Pope Paul VI. Emphasize that evangelization is born of love.

Step Four: Challenge Our Culture

- Clarify that to challenge our culture, we can neither isolate ourselves from it nor reject it completely. Rather, we should affirm and strengthen the good and guide it closer to the truth through example, instruction, and correction.

- Brainstorm some questions with the neophytes during the session. Allow them to suggest responses and sources of information before providing an "answer."

MYSTAGOGY

Step Five: *Make the Good Better*

The fifth step involves taking what's positive in our society and putting it at the service of the gospel. Culture must "be regenerated by an encounter with the Gospel" (*EN* 20). This is our Christian responsibility and is now your responsibility as well. We must do what we can to see that advances in medicine are used at the service of life and not for abortion or euthanasia; to make certain tax dollars that support a massive defense establishment are used to maintain peace in the world; and to find ways to move our economic system toward benefiting members of our society and the world that depend upon us.

What's good in our culture can become better when touched by the transforming power of Christ's good news. People still hunger for love, affection, and salvation. They still crave the good news of Jesus Christ. That's why the Second Vatican Council said we should face the modern world with joy and hope, with the optimism of the transforming gospel.

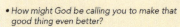

On your own or with a group, create a list of questions you think others may have about the Catholic faith. Include questions you had about the faith before becoming Catholic. Pick one or two questions and research the answers. Use lesson handouts, your notes, the Bible, the *Catechism of the Catholic Church*, and any other resources you have access to. If you don't find an answer by the end of this session, keep searching.

- Describe one area of your life where you really could make a difference to others.
- How can you serve as an example of Christ?

- What are some ways our culture supports the dignity of human life, the sacredness of marriage, the beauty of God's world?
- How might God be calling you to make that good thing even better?

Journey of Faith for Adults: Mystagogy, M8 (826283)
Imprimi Potest: Stephen T. Rehrauer, CSsR, Provincial, Denver Province, the Redemptorists.
Imprimatur: "In accordance with CIC 827, permission to publish has been granted on June 7, 2016, by the Rev. Msgr. Mark S. Rivituso, Vicar General, Archdiocese of St. Louis. Permission to publish is an indication that nothing contrary to Church teaching is contained in this work. It does not imply any endorsement of the opinions expressed in the publication; nor is any liability assumed by this permission."
Journey of Faith for Adults © 2000, 2016 Liguori Publications, Liguori, MO 63057. All rights reserved. No part of this publication may be reproduced, distributed, stored, transmitted, or posted in any form by any means without prior written permission. To order, visit Liguori.org or call 800-325-9521. Liguori Publications, a nonprofit corporation, is an apostolate of the Redemptorists. To learn more about the Redemptorists, visit Redemptorists.com. Contributing Writers: Fr. Alfred McBride, OPraem, and Fr. Michael Parise. Fr. McBride's article was originally published in *Liguorian* magazine, January 1990. Editors of 2016 Journey of Faith: Julia DiSalvo, Joan McKamey, and Denise Bossert. Design: Lorena Mitre Jimenez. Images: Shutterstock. Scripture texts in this work are taken from the *New American Bible*, revised edition © 2010, 1991, 1986, 1970 Confraternity of Christian Doctrine, Washington, D.C., and are used by permission of the copyright owner. All Rights Reserved. No part of the New American Bible may be reproduced in any form without permission in writing from the copyright owner. Excerpts from English translation of the *Catechism of the Catholic Church* for the United States of America © 1994 United States Catholic Conference, Inc.—Libreria Editrice Vaticana; English translation of the *Catechism of the Catholic Church*: Modifications from the Editio Typica © 1997 United States Catholic Conference, Inc.—Libreria Editrice Vaticana. Compliant with *The Roman Missal, Third Edition*. Printed in the United States of America. 20 19 18 17 16 / 5 4 3 2 1. Third Edition.

LIGUORI PUBLICATIONS
A Redemptorist Ministry

Journey of Faith for Adults, Enlightenment and Mystagogy Leader Guide

Journaling

Encourage participants to continue growing in their faith and capturing their faith journey in their journal. Offer some basic suggestions for evangelization, or brainstorm several as a group, if there's time. Then give participants time to respond to the journal prompt on their own.

Closing Prayer

Ask everyone to join hands in a circle. Ask each person to mention one aspect of the RCIA process that has brought him or her closer to God and the Church. Encourage spontaneous prayers of thanksgiving. Remind everyone that our faith journeys continue far beyond this period of formation, and challenge them to support one another in the days, months, and years to come. Conclude with a recitation of the Lord's Prayer and the Glory Be.

If possible, celebrate the conclusion of the program with light refreshments or enjoy a meal together at a favorite restaurant. Have the pastor or deacon present at this gathering bless the meal and members of the RCIA group.

Take-Home

Invite the neophytes to reflect on their RCIA experience in their journal one last time.

Evangelization

Journey of Faith for Adults
Enlightenment and Mystagogy Glossary (alphabetical)

abstinence (E2): Doing without (refraining from) a certain food, drink, or another temporal good for some spiritual benefit. Abstinence from meat is required for all Catholics aged fourteen to fifty-nine on the Fridays of Lent and Ash Wednesday, as determined by the American Catholic bishops (*CIC* 1250–53; *CCC* 2043) (See **fasting**).

almsgiving (E2): Donating money or material goods to the poor and needy as an act of charity or penance (Tobit 12:8–9; Sirach 3:30; Matthew 6:1–4). One of the three main forms of interior penance in the Church (*CCC* 1434).

apostolic (E4): One of the four *marks* or notes of the Church; denoting that the Church "remains, through the successors of St. Peter and the other apostles, in communion of faith and life with her origin" (*CCC* 863; see 857–65). The Catholic Church is apostolic in three ways: (1) "built on 'the foundation of the apostles'"; (2) helped by the Holy Spirit to hand on their teachings as revealed by God; (3) continually guided and sanctified by the successors of the apostles, the college of bishops (*CCC* 857).

begotten (E4): Used to describe the Son, the second divine Person, as "not made" or created but *consubstantial* with the Father and therefore eternal and fully divine (Nicene Creed). He existed with the Father before the beginning of time and received his human nature in the Incarnation for the salvation of all. Jesus' birth and historical presence did not diminish or alter his divinity (see **consubstantial**).

catechesis (M7): "The whole of the efforts within the Church to make disciples, to help people to believe that Jesus is the Son of God…, and to educate and instruct them in this life and thus build up the Body of Christ" (*Catechesi Tradendae*, 1; *CCC* 4). Commonly this refers to formal religious-education and sacramental-preparation programs for children and adults, but it also includes ongoing faith formation within the family and parish (see **evangelization**).

consubstantial (E4): Used by the Council of Nicaea in 325 to indicate that Christ is "one in Being," of the same divine substance, as God the Father. Christ is also *consubstantial* to humanity because he took flesh and became like us "in all things but sin" (Eucharistic Prayer IV; Preface VII of the Sundays in Ordinary Time).

conversion (E3): From the Latin for "turning"; also from the Greek word *metanoia*, meaning a profound and personal change. True conversion involves a complete and authentic change of heart. In Christianity, conversion means to turn away from sin, to come to faith, and to respond with one's whole being to the love of God. Specifically, it refers to an unbaptized nonbeliever's entrance into the Catholic Church.

Corporal Works of Mercy (M6): "Charitable actions by which we come to the aid of our neighbor" (*CCC* 2447). The seven *corporal works of mercy* are directed toward bodily necessities: feed the hungry; give drink to the thirsty; clothe the naked; shelter the homeless; visit the sick; visit the imprisoned; bury the dead.

discernment (M4): From the Latin meaning "to separate apart"; a decision-making process through which we seek to recognize God's will and distinguish between his voice and selfish tendencies or sinful temptations (Romans 12:2; Philippians 1:9–10; 1 John 5:20). "By prayer we can discern 'what is the will of God' and obtain the endurance to do it" (*CCC* 2826). Reason, right judgment, and related actions are guided by the virtue of *prudence* (*CCC* 1806, 1835).

evangelization (M8): From a Greek word meaning "to announce" or "to bring good news"; the process of proclaiming and testifying to the gospel message, especially to those who have not yet heard, or would never otherwise hear, about Jesus Christ. In *Evangelii Nuntiandi*, Pope Paul VI defines it as "bringing the Good News into all the strata of humanity, and through its influence transforming humanity from within and making it new" (*EN* 18). Evangelization may include inspiring Christians to a deeper faith and more active discipleship.

fasting (E2): Freely choosing to limit the kind or quantity of food or drink one consumes as an act of penance or to sacrifice some good to God. One of the three main forms of interior penance in the Church (*CCC* 1434). In the United States, fasting is required for all faithful aged eighteen to fifty-nine on Ash Wednesday and Good Friday and defined as eating only "one full meal, as well as two smaller meals that together are not equal to a full meal," per day (USCCB; see *CCC* 1251–52).

human virtues (M6): Also known as moral or cardinal virtues, "firm attitudes, stable dispositions, habitual perfections of intellect and will that govern our actions, order our passions, and guide our conduct" (*CCC* 1804). Unlike graces and theological virtues, they are acquired through our own efforts, actions, and perseverance in cooperation owith God's grace (*CCC* 1810–11). The four human virtues are *prudence, justice, fortitude,* and *temperance* (see **theological virtues** and **virtue**).

Spiritual Works of Mercy (M6): "Charitable actions by which we come to the aid of our neighbor" (*CCC* 2447). The seven *spiritual works of mercy* are directed toward spiritual necessities: instruct the ignorant; counsel the doubtful; admonish the sinner; bear wrongs patiently; forgive offenses willingly; comfort the afflicted; pray for the living and the dead.

theological virtues (M6): Virtues which "dispose Christians to live in a relationship with the Holy Trinity. They have the One and Triune God for their origin, motive, and object....They are infused by God into the souls of the faithful to make them capable of acting as his children and of meriting eternal life....There are three theological virtues: *faith, hope,* and *charity*" (*CCC* 1812–13, emphasis added; see **human virtues** and **virtue**).

virtue (M6): "An habitual and firm disposition to do the good" (*CCC* 1803). In other words, a nurtured attitude or behavior that makes knowing what is good easy and shapes us into the image and likeness of God. Virtues are *not* merit badges, nor do they prove a person's goodness or worth. (See **human virtues** and **theological virtues**).

witness (M8): The act of a believer living out their faith in Jesus Christ, the gospel, and his Church through his or her thoughts, words, and deeds even when those actions result in personal sacrifice or the hostility of others. Christian witness reveals the truth and testifies to the individual's faith.